A HOG ON ICE

*And Other
Curious Expressions*

A HOG ON ICE

And Other Curious
Expressions

Charles Earle Funk, Litt.D.

With Illustrations by
Tom Funk

HARPER COLOPHON BOOKS
Harper & Row, Publishers
New York, Cambridge, Philadelphia, San Francisco
London, Mexico City, São Paulo, Singapore, Sydney

A hardcover edition of this book was published by Harper & Row, Publishers, Inc.

A HOG ON ICE AND OTHER CURIOUS EXPRESSIONS. Copyright 1948 by Harper & Row, Publishers, Inc. All rights reserved. Printed in the United States of America. No part of this book may be used or reproduced in any manner whatsoever without written permission except in the case of brief quotations embodied in critical articles and reviews. For information address Harper & Row, Publishers, Inc., 10 East 53rd Street, New York, N.Y. 10022. Published simultaneously in Canada by Fitzhenry & Whiteside Limited, Toronto.

First HARPER COLOPHON edition published 1985.

Library of Congress Cataloging in Publication Data

Funk, Charles Earle, 1881–1957.
   A hog on ice and other curious expressions.

   (Harper colophon books)
   Includes index.
   1. English language—Terms and phrases. 2. English language—Etymology.
I. Title.
PE1689.F76   1985   428.1   84-48646
ISBN 0-06-091259-6 (pbk.)

88 89 90   20 19 18 17 16 15 14 13 12 11

To the memory
of my mother,
Cynthia Ellen Funk

FOREWORD

CURIOSITY about the origin of an expression that my mother frequently used started the investigation which has led to the contents of this book. Whenever she saw a pompous person strutting down the street, a girl leading the way to a restaurant table without heeding the head waiter's guidance, a young man with hat atilt jauntily striding along without a care in the world, a baby who had just learned to walk ignoring the outstretched hand of its mother, such a person, she always said with a toss of her own head, was "as independent as a hog on ice." She meant cockily independent, supremely confident, beholden to no one.

Now my mother was born and brought up on a farm in southern Ohio, in a region wholly given over to farms. She knew full well that a hapless hog that found itself upon the ice would be utterly helpless, unable to rise, its feet sprawled out in all directions. So why did she use this expression with such a contrary meaning? Of course, I never thought to ask her while she was living; I doubt now, in fact, that she could have told me. It was a saying that she had picked up from her own elders, and they in turn from the generation that preceded.

The homely expression, though not extinct, is rarely heard nowadays; so it was not until a few years ago that I found that my wife, whose forebears dwelt in eastern Massachusetts from Puritan days, was just as cognizant of the simile as I—and knew no more of its origin. Then, of course, I turned to the collection of phrase books on my shelves—to Holt's *Phrase Origins*, FitzGerald's *Words and*

Phrases, Brewer's *Dictionary of Phrase and Fable*, Walsh's *Handy-Book of Literary Curiosities*, Hyamson's *Dictionary of English Phrases*, Apperson's *English Proverbs and Proverbial Phrases*, and others old and new—but none even listed the saying. The dictionaries were next to be consulted. Of all of them, not one listed and defined the expression as a whole, though the Supplement, published in 1933, to the huge *Oxford English Dictionary* came within an ace of so doing. There, under "hog" it listed the phrase, "like, or as, a hog on ice," giving it the definition, "denoting awkwardness or insecurity." It credited the saying to the United States and gave two quotations showing its use. The first, from a Vermont paper of 1894, really illustrated the definition, for it pertained to a certain horse which, upon a racetrack, would be as awkward as a hog upon the ice. The second, taken from Carl Sandburg's "The Windy City," from *Slabs of the Sunburnt West*, read: "Chicago fished from its depths a text: Independent as a hog on ice." The editors slipped, however, in the inclusion of this quotation under the definition, for it does not fit. A reading of the entire poem shows that Sandburg used the full phrase, "independent as a hog on ice," in the sense that my mother knew it—to indicate that "the Windy City" was quite able to stand upon its own feet, had supreme confidence and self-assurance.

My next step, then, was to refer to the vast resources of the New York Public Library, to enlist the aid of some of its researchers, and especially to consult the complete file of *Notes & Queries*, the British monthly publication that since 1850 has been the recognized medium for the exchange of antiquarian information among its readers. I found nothing. Subsequently, I may say here, direct appeal to the readers of *Notes & Queries* was equally non-productive, nor did the larger resources of the Chicago Public Library, extended through the courtesy of its librarian, Mr. Carl B. Roden, yield anything that I did not already know.

In the meantime I had been questioning my friends and acquaintances. Some, especially of a younger generation, had never heard the expression, but almost all those within my own generation or older were familiar with it, or had heard it in childhood. Upon further inquiry I found that the localities in which these people had known the phrase included all the northern states from Maine to Illinois; later, through correspondence, I was able to add many of the southern states, though in Georgia "pig" was more familiar than "hog." Perhaps by chance, none to whom I wrote west of the Mississippi had ever heard the expression. Parenthetically, one friend recalled from his youth an old codger who, when asked how he was, would respond, "Oh, just as independent as a hog on ice; if I can't stand up I can lay down." No one else knew this additional line.

The search was momentarily halted in its early stages because, having no farm experience myself, I could not positively state from my own knowledge, in answer to a question, that a hog was actually helpless upon the ice. The questioner had heard, he said, that by virtue of its sharp hoofs a hog had no trouble whatever in maneuvering itself upon ice. So I sent an inquiry to the Bureau of Animal Industry, U. S. Department of Agriculture, to make certain. The reply, from Mr. John H. Zeller, Senior Animal Husbandman, In Charge Swine Investigations, reads, in part:

The facts are that a hog on a smooth icy surface cannot move about in a normal manner. The pads on the feet are smooth and offer no resistance to slippery or smooth icy surfaces. His feet slide out from under him, the legs will either spread as the animal sprawls out on the ice, or they will be drawn under him. In either case, after several attempts to arise, he refuses to try to get on his feet. The hog usually has to be skidded or dragged off the ice to a firm footing before he attempts to move about in the usual manner.

So, reassured on this point, my search proceeded.

The fact that the gelid independent hog was known, apparently, throughout all the eastern states some eighty or more years ago, made me wonder whether it may have been connected in some way with a historical episode. Digging back, I recalled that after the Revolutionary War our newly created republic had its independence, all right, but that, through internal squabbles and lack of credit abroad, for many years this independence had very nearly the grace and security of a hog on ice. Perhaps some satirist of that period had coined the phrase, and perhaps it had been disseminated through a political song. Again the resources of the library were called upon, and more letters were sent—this time to historians and to writers of historical fiction. Again the library was non-productive—no satire and no song or ballad could be found in which the phrase appeared. The historians, without exception, had heard the saying. Professor Charles Beard found my theory of a Tory satirical origin interesting and plausible, but could offer no clue; Arthur Schlesinger, Jr., did not recall its occurrence in any of his readings upon the Jacksonian period. Two other eminent scholars, one born in Illinois, the other in Indiana—had always vaguely supposed, from childhood, that the saying had somehow arisen from the meat-packing industry in Chicago or in Cincinnati, without recalling that, prior to about 1880 when refrigeration was introduced, meat was preserved by salting, drying, corning, smoking, pickling, or the like, but not by freezing. Furthermore, if the saying were associated with packing, a sheep or a cow when frozen would be just as independent as a hog.

But the historical novelist, Kenneth Roberts, drew my attention away from the probability of American coinage, for he replied to my request by saying that he had always known the expression, that it was commonly used by his grandmother in her home in New Hampshire when he was young. Then he added: "A lot of expressions which I later found to be old English were in common use in our family—which came from Godalming near Stratford-on-Avon in the early 1630s. So I suspect that 'independent as a hog on ice' is older than you think." He gave his own explanation of the simile: "I strongly suspect the phrase was applied to people who were idiotically independent: that a man who was *that* independent was getting himself exactly nowhere, like a spread-eagled hog."

Because two acquaintances who were born in Ireland had told me that they had heard the expression in the "Ould counthry," I had already briefly considered Ireland as the possible source of the saying—its transmission throughout all of the eastern United States could readily be accounted for by the great Irish immigration of 1820-1840 into all of the eastern states. But I had discarded the likelihood, for, as Padraic Colum reminded me, there is no ice in Ireland and hogs are called pigs. I had concluded that my earlier informants, who had been brought to this country when very young, had heard it here and assumed that it was Irish. But now, along with Roberts' opinion, came a letter from Peter Tamany of San Francisco, notable collector of unusual words, in which he said that his mother, a woman of seventy-five, born near Macroom, County Cork, had often heard the saying as a young girl. Then a chance acquaintance in New York City, a man of sixty-five, hailing from Belfast and still owning land near that city, told me that, though one hears the expression rarely now in Northern Ireland, it is still well known among the older folks. Then, too, H. L. Mencken, who wrote that he had known it in Baltimore from boyhood, said that he had always had the impression that it was of Irish origin. Professor Harold W. Thompson, folklorist and writer, also thought it likely to have been an Irish importation, and then added—"but what would the Irish immigrant know about ice? Would the Irish peasant ever have hogs on ice? Also, why is a hog on ice independent? Is it because he has attained the dignity of death?"

The net result of these latter opinions was that I abandoned my earlier thought of an American origin. Despite the evidence of use in Ireland, however, I agreed with Colum, Thompson, and others that probability of an Irish origin was not likely. Hence, in Ireland as in America, it must have been an importation. But from where? Sir William Craigie, co-editor of the Oxford English Dictionary, thought it most improbable that England could have been the source, both because of the rarity of ice and because "pig" is also British use, rather than "hog." Sir St. Vincent Troubridge advanced similar arguments and, like all previous English acquaintances whom I had consulted, had never heard the expression in England. But, at about that stage of my search, I began to get returns from another direction.

A fellow worker, an Englishwoman, interested in my search had been in correspondence with her brother, Leslie Campbell Stark, living in the north of England. Though he was not himself acquainted with the expression, he began to make inquiries and learned, surprisingly, that the usage was known in northern England, especially among the old-timers and more especially among his Scottish acquaintances. This news altered the entire trend of my thought and caused me to take up again a line of reasoning that, early in the search, had been abandoned as wholly untenable. Possibly, though no one now could give the reason, the expression was of Scottish origin. If so, this would explain its occurrence in Northern Ireland and its spread in the United States. My mother was of Scottish descent, and perhaps—though I have not attempted to pursue this theory—the saying has persisted particularly among other such families. And if the expression was Scottish, then perhaps the allusion to a swine was indirect. I might say here also that it is by no means unknown for a word or saying to survive in America that has long been obsolete in England; the incongruity of this saying would especially appeal to American or Irish ears, lending strength to its survival.

If one looks in the dictionary—an unabridged dictionary—he will see that, in the game of curling, a Scottish game played upon ice, the word "hog" is used to describe a curling stone under certain conditions. That is, when a player does not give his stone sufficient impetus to cause it to slide beyond a certain distance, that stone, when it comes to rest, is called a "hog." No explanation of the name has been given, but the Century Dictionary, published originally in 1889, says of the entry, "Origin obscure; by some identified with hog (i. e., swine), as 'laggard stones that manifest a pig-like indolence,' or, it might be thought, in allusion to the helplessness of a hog on ice, there being in the United States an ironical simile, 'as independent as a hog on ice!'" Incidentally, this appearance of the phrase in the Century Dictionary is its earliest occurrence in print; at least, no earlier appearance has been found. The Century did not list the phrase separately nor offer any further explanation of it.

Back toward the beginning of my search, I had thought for awhile that this curling stone afforded an ideal explanation of the phrase, that the "hog," lying indolently upon the course, was free and independent, by its immobile state blocking the way of subsequent stones to be played, forming a hazard. But the thought was short-lived, for when I read over the rules of the game I saw that the stone does not constitute a hazard, for the "hog" is removed from the course as soon as it comes to rest. It blocks nothing and attains no independence! Reluctantly, therefore, I had dismissed this explanation of the phrase from further consideration.

But now, after tracing the simile back to a probable Scottish origin, it seemed feasible to look again into this game. Its antiquity is not known, but it dates at least to the early sixteenth century, for of a number of early crude stones that have been found in the beds and along the shores of Scottish rivers and ponds, one has the date 1509 cut in its side. No earlier reference in literature has been found, however, than 1620, and no prescribed set of rules is known to have been drawn up or followed until another century had passed. So, because no writer mentioned the sport, it is apparent that curling, like many other games started very humbly, perhaps among a group of boys who, at first, had improvised a game of bowls on the ice, using small stones as the pins and larger ones in place of balls. Perhaps, because round stones to roll over the ice could not be found, they used flattened stones that could be slid. Older lads or men taking over the game would then undoubtedly have introduced refinements and hazards unthought of by boys—ultimately leading through the centuries to the exacting rules and highly polished, heavy stones, rounded, as of today. But in its early days I think the method of play had local differences wherever the game was played—such, at least, has been the history of most games. When, later, teams of players were organized and competition was introduced, then some agreement had to be reached as to method of play. But, again, if other sports are any criterion—and we need only to look back over the few brief years in the history of baseball or basketball for an example—curling undoubtedly underwent many changes before the rules of the eighteenth century were put down on paper.

Hence, though my conclusion cannot be proved, I think that sometime during the early centuries of the game, perhaps by accident one of the awkward, heavy stones did not have enough momentum to carry it to its destination and it stopped halfway along the course. I think that someone made the suggestion that it be allowed to stay there as an extra hazard, and I think that, because of its unwieldiness and its inertness, becoming partly frozen into the ice, some player with a sense of humor likened it to a hog—and the name stuck. If this hypothesis be correct, then the very fact that the stone occupied a central position, showing no regard to its interference with subsequent players, like an automobile driver who "hogs" the center of a road, made it appear self-assured, cocky, and independent, and thus gave rise to the humorous simile that came down through the centuries. Perhaps—to explain the later development leading to the present removal of the "hog"—there may have been a tendency among some players to encumber the course with their curling stones deliberately, thus blocking the game. So, perhaps, the rule was made that a stone must traverse five sixths of the course, as at present—passing a line upon the ice still known as the "hog score"—before it would be permitted to remain on the ice and exert its independence. This theory, as the Century Dictionary suggests, would give us "laggard stones that manifest a pig-like indolence."

No one has tried to make an individual collection of all the common sayings in the English language; there are thousands of them. They have come from all the trades and professions; they have come from the courts of kings and from beggars' hovels; they have come from churches and cathedrals and they have come from gambling hells and bawdy houses. A large number have come from the sea, because England existed through maritime trade for many centuries and the speech of her sailors has become commonplace in every British port. Many have come from the battlefield or the arts of warfare; others from the hunt or the fisherman's boat. Many have come down to us from the loom and the spindle, because weaving, once introduced into England from the Continent, became a staple industry, practiced throughout the kingdom. The farmer's field and his livestock and the housewife and her domestic chores have supplied many more. But aside from these serious occupational sources, a lesser number have been derived from games and sports. These latter include the pastimes of children, the rough outdoor and indoor sports and games of boys and men, and games of skill and chance.

These sayings, whatever the source, have become folk sayings, adopted into the common speech of English-speaking peoples generally, for they became part of the language. Thus, we in America, though we have added and are still adding many more expressions peculiar to this country which will pass on to our children's children, are using phrases and sayings in our common speech that hark back to the days of the Wars of the Roses and the House of Tudor. Along with them are sayings from other languages which also have become English folk sayings. A few of these have come, apparently, from Scandinavian sources—such as, "to run the gantlet," "to cook one's goose," and, perhaps, "to pay through the nose"; a number have come from France, both from the common speech and from French literature, which is not surprising when one considers that for two centuries after the Norman Conquest it was a toss-up between French or English as the common language and that French was the court language for three centuries more. Some of the sayings that we use every day are nothing more than English translations of Latin, Greek, or Hebrew—and this, too, is not surprising, for Latin, until recent centuries was the literary language of all learned, scholarly people throughout Europe, and even to the days of our own grandparents every schoolboy had to be proficient in both Latin and Greek; and, of course, the Old Testament, from which we have many familiar sayings, was a Hebrew document.

Many of these sayings are nothing more than figurative applications of commonplace utterances. They require no explanation, because almost no one's imagination is so weak that the allusion is not immediately evident. In my study I have discarded the obvious and have considered only those that, for one reason or another, I regard as curious or especially picturesque or out of the ordinary. Some, of modern vintage, have been included for perhaps no better reason than that they have struck my fancy, or because I thought it worth while to record what I know or surmise to be the explanations back of their use. An amusing expression, either one that is incongruous or that involves a play upon words, is quick to seize the popular fancy and seems to live until there is scarcely more than a ghost left of the original circumstance that caused its popularity. The clue leading to its source many depend upon some former dialectal word

or expression, or upon some ancient practice among certain tradesmen, or upon some obscure local event or custom, or upon some
long-forgotten diversion. Such sayings I have tried to trace. These
threads provide the reasons for such old phrases as "higher then
Gilderoy's kite," "to leave in the lurch," "to kick the bucket," "from
pillar to post," and scores of others. But in some expressions no
trace remains by which we can step with any confidence to the
source. No one knows, with certainty, what was originally meant
by the admonition, "to mind one's *p*'s and *q*'s," nor why, when things
were neatly arranged, they were said to be "in apple-pie order," nor
why a person with a broad smile was said to "grin like a Cheshire
cat." These and others in this category must have been readily understood at one time, and the allusions must have been so clear and
definite that no one thought it necessary to describe them. Each
must have been based upon a common practice, an incident, a spec-
tacle, or the like that was familiar to all among whom the saying was
first introduced; but, even as today, no one then made a written
record because no one had any reason to believe that the saying
would persist and become commonplace.

Does any family, for example, make a record of the words or
sayings peculiar to it? I doubt it, though sometimes they are apt and
worthy of perpetuation. One such, still used among the third generation of a family that I was once privileged to know, might have
been written, from the sound, "peebidess." It was used, variously,
to designate an ambitious but impoverished family or community,
or something vainly pretentious, or even something that had once
been fine but had become bedraggled or faded—anything, that is,
deserving of commiseration. Eventually I learned that the first
generation of users—five clever sisters—had coined it for secret conversation, using initials: "*P.* but *S.*," poor but struggling.

One does not expect to be able to discover who the one individual
was, in any given instance, who first took an innocent remark or
incident and gave it a metaphorical twist. We say that some came
from Shakespeare or Spenser or Chaucer, but it is really not very
likely that these or other writers would take the chance that their
readers or audience would grasp the point of some wholly new

witticism. All that we can do, then, is to trace the written record back and thus, in most instances, find out approximately when the saying came into use. (We do not often find that, as with the independent hog, two or three centuries have passed before some writer has made use of the saying.)

So what I have done herein is to take those curious sayings that I have selected, give to each the figurative meaning that it has acquired, show, whenever possible, how that meaning has come about, and make an approximate estimate of the time it came into use in English speech. Occasionally, to lend vividness to the account, I have taken the reader back into ancient ways and practices, or I have quoted from old texts. The intent has been, with due regard to accuracy, to use such means as were available to enable the reader to retain the sources of these sayings in his memory. To this end, also, the aid of my nephew, Tom Funk, was enlisted to scatter some of his black-and-white "spots" throughout the text.

The collection ranges over some two thousand years of time, for along with curious sayings of former centuries are included some coined within recent decades—"hitting on all six," "on the nose," "behind the eight ball," "Bronx cheer" are examples. Here again, with a few exceptions, the actual origins are elusive. Someone must have devised the gesture of touching his nose as an indication that the timing was exact; someone must have been the first to designate a peculiarly raucous, derisive sound as a "Bronx cheer"; it may be a natural way among automobile mechanics to say that a smoothly running engine is "hitting on all four," or "hitting on all six," depending upon the number of its cylinders, but someone must have been the first to take this and use it figuratively. I have been unable to learn who were the authors of these and like phrases, though it is likely that they are living. Positive information from any reader will be appreciated.

The material for many of these sketches has been collected over a number of years in connection with other work, collected through correspondence, through newspaper clippings, through the files of *Notes & Queries*, through encyclopedias and dictionaries, and through scores of other reference works which have been checked one with another. I am especially indebted to the Oxford English

Dictionary and to the Dictionary of American English for references
to early literary use of many of the expressions discussed and for
various quotations of such use, and to the former, in many instances,
for valuable etymological clues. In a few instances, Apperson's
English Proverbs and Proverbial Phrases has supplied references
to earlier usage than had been found by the editors of either of those
dictionaries.

A HOG ON ICE

*And Other
Curious Expressions*

in a blue funk

It would be interesting if, through family records, I could bring an unsuspected source into view which would explain why this expression means "in a state of dire panic," or from another record determine why a stooge for an auctioneer, one who makes fictitious bids to stimulate higher bids, is called a "Peter Funk"; but, alas, no such records are known. An actual Peter Funk who thus served an auctioneer may have lived, in some part of the United States, but the unusually full record of the American family from 1710 to 1900 has no mention of such an individual. The English phrase, "in a funk," was Oxford slang back in the middle of the eighteenth century, and seems to have been borrowed from a Flemish phrase, "in de fonck siin," which also meant "in a state of panic"; but no one has been  able to figure out why the Flemish *fonck* meant "panic." Perhaps some ancestor, for the early American branch spelled the name "Funck" and came from lands bordering the Flemings, may have lived in such panic that his name, slightly misspelled, became a synonym for great fear. No one can say.

"Blue" was inserted into the phrase about a hundred years after the Oxford adoption. The adjective had long been used to mean "extreme," and its addition merely intensified the state of panic ascribed to the phrase.

Incidentally, the first literary mention of the mythical "Peter Funk" is in the book by Asa Green, *The Perils of Pearl Street*, published in 1834. The book is a humorous narrative of mercantile life in New York City and, obviously, the author invented the names of most of the characters he describes. Possibly this name was also invented, though the author says that Peter Funk was a name familiar to generations of merchants.

to put the kibosh on

To put an end to; to stop; to dispose of. One thinks of this as being modern slang, in use only a few years, but readers of Dickens, if they remember *Sketches by Boz*, may recall the sketch, "Seven Dials." This is a description of a squalid locality in London, so benighted that even the "ladies" were usually engaged in fisticuffs. One such battle was egged on by a young potboy, who, as Dickens wrote it, roared to one of the "ladies," "Hooroar, put the kye-bosk on her, Mary!" That sketch was published back in 1836, so our "modern slang" is somewhat more than a hundred years old.

There has been considerable speculation about the origin of the word "kibosh." A correspondent to *Notes & Queries* some years ago advanced the theory that it was of Yiddish origin meaning eighteen pence, and began as a term used in auctions, as an increase in a bid. Recently, another correspondent to the same publication suggested that it may be a corruption of the Italian *capuce*, a tin lid, and that it may have been employed by street vendors of ice-cream—"Put the kibosh on," meant to put the lid back on the container.

But I am indebted to Padraic Colum, well-known Irish author, for what I take to be the true explanation. In a letter to me he says: " 'Kibosh,' I believe, means 'the cap of death' and it is always used in that sense—'He put the kibosh on it.' In Irish it could be written 'cie bais'—the last word pronounced 'bosh,' the genitive of 'bas,' death."

to knock (or beat) the tar out of

We use this with the meaning, to beat, whip, or belabor without mercy. Though credited to the United States and with no earlier record of use than the twentieth century, I think it likely that the expression may have been carried to this country by some Scottish or north-of-England sheepherder who may have used it in a literal sense. Many centuries ago it was learned that a sore on a sheep, as from an accidental cut in shearing, could be protected against the festering bites of flies if smeared with tar. In fact, back in 1670, the proverb is recorded by John Ray, "Ne're lose a hog (later, a sheep) for a half-penny-worth of tarre." But when tar once gets embedded into a sheep's wool, its removal is difficult. So I surmise that our present saying was first used in its literal sense, to beat a sheep's side for the removal of tar.

hell-bent for election

"Hell-bent," an American term, means so determined as to be regardless of the consequences, even hell itself. An article in *Knickerbocker Magazine* in an issue of 1835 describes a band of Indians as "hell-bent on carnage." The present "all out" is a mild substitute for the same thing. But "hell-bent for election" means speed, speed so great as to be heedlessly reckless. The meaning seems to be derived from the political race made by Edward Kent, in 1840, for election to the governorship of Maine. He was a Whig, and, though Maine was then normally Democratic, he had served as governor for one term, had been defeated for re-election by John Fairfield, and was again running against Fairfield in 1840. The Whigs were determined to win; they were "hell-bent for the election" of Kent and probably used that slogan in the campaign, for their victory was celebrated by a song that ran, in part:

> *Oh have you heard how old Maine went?*
> *She went hell-bent for Governor Kent,*
> *And Tippecanoe and Tyler, too!*

spick and span

For the past two hundred years we have been using this to mean very trim and smart, thoroughly neat and orderly, having the appearance of newness, but for the two hundred years preceding that, or from the middle of the sixteenth century to the middle of the eighteenth century, the phrase was always "spick and span new," and had no other meaning than absolutely and wholly new.

The phrase has had an interesting history. It started, so far as the records show, about 1300 as just "span-new," meaning perfectly new, or as new as a freshly cut chip, for "span," in olden days, meant a chip. At that time, chips were used for spoons, so "span-new" really meant a newly cut spoon, one that had not yet been soiled by use.

"Spick" was not added until late in the sixteenth century, presumably for no better reason than alliteration. A "spick" really meant a splinter, or, also, a spike. Actually, it had no particular meaning when added to "span-new," but it would be interesting if I could say that the original purpose of the "spick," or splinter, was to impale meat, as we use a fork today, when the "span" was laid aside.

cock-and-bull story

The French have a phrase, *coq-à-l'âne*—literally, cock to the donkey—which they use in exactly the same sense as we use cock-and-bull; concocted and incredible; fantastic. A cock-and-bull story is one that stretches the imaginations somewhat beyond the limits of credulity. Many learned attempts have been made, both in  French and English lore, to discover the precise origin of the phrase, which has appeared in English literature since about 1600, but nothing has yet been determined. Probably it came from a folk tale, one concerning a cock and a donkey, in France, and a cock and a bull, in England. A writer back in 1660, Samuel Fisher, speaks of a cock and a bull being metamorphosed into one animal, but more likely in the original fable the two barnyard animals engaged in conversation. As no farmer would believe that such conversation was possible, he would be apt to label any incredible tale as a "cock-and-bull story."

not dry behind the ears

As innocent and unsophisticated as a babe. A saying that came directly from the farm, where many others have also arisen, for it alludes to a newly born animal, as a colt or a calf, on which the last spot to become dry after birth is the little depression behind either ear. The figurative use seems to be wholly American, too homely to have attained literary pretensions, but undoubtedly in familiar use through the past hundred years or longer.

in the bag

With success assured; all over but the shouting. The saying is new; that is, it has become generally known throughout America, where it originated, since about 1920. In card games or the like, the person doing the playing may use it when he wishes to free his partner's mind from anxiety. An earlier expression with the same inference was "all wrapped up"; that is, in allusion to merchandise, success was assured and merely awaited delivery. When paper bags succeeded wrapping paper for the holding of groceries or the like, the later saying succeeded the older.

to be (or go) woolgathering

To be engaged in trivial employment; to indulge in aimless reverie. Though this expression has long had such figurative meanings, its origin was literal; people did actually wander in a seemingly aimless manner over the countryside gathering the fragments of wool left by passing sheep on bushes or fences against which they brushed. Such people were "woolgatherers," and it is likely that in some countries children are so employed today. The figurative sense was in use as long ago as the middle of the sixteenth century, as in Thomas Wilson's *The arte of rhetorique*, "Hackyng & hemmyng as though our wittes and our senses were a woll gatheryng."

to cool one's heels

To be kept waiting, as when you have a train to catch, but must see a prospective customer who keeps you nervously fuming in his outer office. The figurative meaning dates back to the early seventeenth century, and the phrase, though the evidence is scant, was apparently preceded by the more literal, "to cool one's hoofs." Here, the allusion is to a draft horse or saddle horse which takes advantage of a period of rest by lying down. "To kick one's heels" is a later variant, from about the middle of the eighteenth century, with the same meaning, except that impatience is always implied. Here the allusion is to a restless horse which, when kept standing, kicks its stall. "To kick up one's heels" has two meanings, each different, and having no similarity with the foregoing. In one sense the phrase means playfulness, especially that of an elderly person who momentarily affects the careless spirits of a child. Here the allusion is to a horse which, turned out to pasture, frisks about briefly with the careless abandon of a colt. In the other sense it means to trip a person; that is, to cause the person to kick up his own heels by falling flat.

to ride the high horse; on one's high horse

Away back in the fourteenth century John Wyclif records that in a royal pageant persons of high rank were mounted on "high" horses, meaning that they rode the so-called  "great horses," or heavy chargers used in battle or tournament. Hence, the use of such a horse was presumptive evidence that its rider was, or considered himself to be, a person of superiority or arrogance. The custom died, but the expression remains. "To ride the high horse" means to affect arrogance or superiority, to act pretentiously. From it we have the derived phrase, "on one's high horse," which we use descriptively of a person who affects to scorn those who or that which he feigns to believe beneath his notice.

to have two strings to one's bow

Anciently, the bowman who went forth to battle was ill prepared unless he carried two or more bowstrings. Otherwise he would be utterly useless if the one on his bow were to snap. Thus, probably long before Cardinal Wolsey recorded it in 1524, the expression had acquired the figurative meaning still in use, to have two (or more) resources, or to be prepared with alternate plans for carrying out one's intent.

dyed in the wool

Probably back beyond the days of Jacob—who gave his favorite son, Joseph, " a coat of many colors"—it was known that if the wool were dyed before it was made up into yarn, or while it was still raw wool, the color would be more firmly fixed. The figurative sense—to have one's habits or traits so deeply ingrained as to be inflexible—seems not to have been used in England before the late sixteenth century, for a writer of that period thought he had to explain his meaning when he used it. This was odd, for England was largely dependent upon her textile industry then and earlier for her existence, and any allusion to that industry should have been immediately evident to any Englishman.

all over but the shouting

Success is so certain that applause only is lacking. Though the earliest appearance of the saying in print appears to be in the works of the Welsh writer on sports, Charles James Apperley, in 1842, to my notion the expression has the earmarks of American origin. I would infer that the real origin might have pertained to a hotly contested early American election. The results would not be positively known until the ballots were all counted, but one of the parties might be so sure of success—through the sentiments of the voters at the polls, for instance—as to have little doubt of the outcome. With him, the election was over and nothing was lacking but the plaudits of the multitude.

to fall between two stools

The French is, *être assis entre deux chaises*, literally, to be seated between two seats, and the meaning, as in English, is to fail through lack of decision. It cannot be determined, but the French is probably the older saying, the English no more than a translation. The earliest English record is in John Gower's *Confessio amantis*, of 1390, "Betwen tuo Stoles lyth the fal, Whan that men wenen best to sitte (Between two stools lieth the fall when one thinks one is sitting best)." The allusion is, of course, to the concrete fact: a man seeing a seat at his left rear and one at his right rear, is likely to miss each of them.

to take the bull by the horns

If you have inadvertently insulted your employer's best customer, you must eventually "take the bull by the horns"—screw your courage to the sticking point, and tell the boss what happened; for we use the expression to mean, to face an unpleasant, difficult, or dangerous situation with such courage as one can muster and with the hope that such decisive action may avert disastrous consequences.

In all probability this saying is derived from the Spanish bullfighting, from that division of the contest in which, after planting their darts into the neck of the maddened bull, the *banderilleros* endeavor to tire him out by urging him to rush at their cloaks, by leaping upon his back, and by seizing him by the horns to hold his nose down. But possibly the saying came down from the brutal old English sport of bull-running, as it was called. This sport originated, it is said, in the reign of King John, or about the year 1200, and in the little market town of Stamford, Lincolnshire. Annually upon the thirteenth of November and promptly at eleven o'clock a bull was turned loose in the market place. Men and boys, then, with clubs and dogs pursued the animal, trying to drive it upon the bridge over the Welland River. There, those with courage tried to seize the furious beast and tumble it into the river, grasping it by the horns to do so. When the bull swam ashore to adjacent meadows, miry at that season, the run was continued until both the mob and the bull, spattered with mud, were utterly fatigued. The bull was then slaughtered and its meat sold, at a low price, to those who had participated in the run. The sport was finally abolished in 1840.

to feather one's nest

To provide for one's comfort; especially, for comfort in later life by amassing wealth. The import is to the practice of many birds which, after building their nests, pluck down from their breasts to provide a soft lining that will be comfortable during the long hours of setting upon the eggs. The oldest English literary occurrence is in 1553, but a more typical example is that used in 1590 by the young poet, Robert Greene, "She sees thou hast fethred thy nest, and hast crowns in thy purse."

to ring the changes

To state something over and over again in different ways. It comes from the art of bell ringing, which first came into popularity in the seventeenth century. A "change" means the order in which a series of bells are rung. Thus, with a series of 4 bells, as in the Westminster chimes, it is possible to ring 24 changes without once repeating the order in which the bells are struck. With 5 bells, 120 changes can be rung, for the variety increases enormously with the increase in the number of bells. With 12 bells, the greatest number used in change ringing, the huge figure of 479,001,600 changes is possible—possible, but not probable. The greatest number ever actually rung upon church bells is reported to have been 16,000 changes, and this took somewhat more than nine hours—and the physical exhaustion of the ringers. All the possible changes with any series of bells constitutes a "peal," but when we use the expression in the figurative sense, we convey the idea of repetition *ad nauseum* by saying, "She rang *all* the changes."

to wear one's heart on one's sleeve

Though Shakespeare was the first to use this saying, thus indicating an ostentatious display of one's limitless devotion, he was merely adapting another phrase current in his day and which he himself used in an earlier play. It was Iago, in *Othello*, who wore his heart on his sleeve, professing a devotion to his master, Othello, which, with him, was altogether feigned. The usual phrase of that period was to pin (a thing) upon one's sleeve. Shakespeare uses this in *Love's Labor's Lost*, where Biron, speaking of Boyet, says, "This gallant pins the wenches on his sleeve," meaning that Boyet is openly devoted to all wenches.

to know beans

This is usually in the negative; one who doesn't know beans is appallingly ignorant or is wholly unacquainted with the subject under discussion. It is likely that the expression arose from some story that went the rounds in America early in the nineteenth century, but, if so, the story has been lost. It is possible, however, that it arose from some dispute over the cowpea, which, despite the name, is more nearly related to the bean than to the pea and which is often called either the black-eyed bean or the black-eyed pea. But, as Walsh suggests, it is more likely that the reference was to the famous city of Boston, "the home of the bean and the cod," the city of culture, the hub of the universe, where it would be a mark of the sheerest ignorance not to know that Boston baked beans, to be fit to eat, must be made of that variety of small white bean known as "pea bean."

It might be, of course, that this American expression was contracted from the British phrase, "to know how many beans make five"—a silly saying that probably got started several centuries ago by having children learn to count by using beans. When little Cecil got far enough advanced to know how many beans made five, he was very intelligent and well informed, which is what the phrase means.

to put (or set) the cart before the horse

To get the order of things reversed, as to give the answer to a riddle while attempting to give the riddle. This common occurrence must also have been common among the ancient Greeks and Romans, for they also had sayings that agree with ours. The Greeks said, "Hysteron proteron," which meant, literally, the latter the former.

The Romans said, "Currus bovem trahit præpostere," or, literally, the plow is drawn by the oxen in reversed position, and this, as a matter of record, is the way the saying first appeared in English. It is found in Dan Michel's *Ayenbite of Inwyt* (*Remorse of Conscience*), a translation by Dan Michel of a French treatise, written by Laurentius Gallus, in 1279, into the dialect of Kent. Michel renders it "Moche uolk of religion zetteth the zouly be-uore the oksen, (Many religious folk set the plow before the oxen)." In the course of the next two hundred years the English version became the present usage.

It must be recalled, of course, as the artist has shown, that some coal mines, cut as tunnels, are so laid out that a coal cart, when filled, could go by gravity out to the open, the horse or mule being needed chiefly to get the empty cart back to the face of the mine. But actually, on the outward trip, the horse is reversed in its shafts to act as a holdback, keeping the full cart from going too rapidly.

small fry

We use this humorously when speaking of young children. Our ancestors for the past four hundred years have done the same, so the humor is somewhat antique. But the joke is on us, because even in the remote day when we borrowed "fry" from the Norse, it meant the children of a man's family. That meaning died out, however, and the present humorous usage is rather a reference to the numerous progeny (or "fry") of salmon. And even now it implies a considerable number of small children.

of the first water

Water, in the sense of luster or brilliancy as applied to diamonds or pearls, is presumably a meaning that was borrowed, in translation, from Arabic gem traders, for the same expression is found in other European languages. Three centuries ago, diamonds were graded as first water, second water, or third water, those of the first water being white stones of the highest quality. The old method of grading died out before 1850, but "of the first water" remains in the language to indicate that the person or thing to which it is applied exemplifies the perfection of a flawless diamond. Even "a liar of the first water," would surpass all other liars in the perfection of his falsehoods.

Hobson's choice

The choice of taking what is offered or having nothing at all. Thomas Hobson, who died in 1630 at the ripe age of eighty-five or eighty-six, was a carrier, with his stables in Cambridge and his route running to London, sixty miles away. He was popular among the students of the university, for he drove his own stage over the long route, becoming well known to his passengers, and also because he was entrusted with the privilege of carrying the university mail. Not all the students kept riding horses, and Hobson had extra horses in his stables which could be hired by them, thus becoming, it is said, the first in England to have conducted such a business. But Hobson, according to an article by Steele in the *Spectator* a hundred years later, had observed that the young men rode too hard, so, rather than risk the ruin of his best horses, which were most in demand, he made an unvarying rule that no horse be taken except in its proper turn—that, or none at all. "Every customer," said Steele, "was alike well served according to his chance, and every horse ridden with the same justice."

Hobson's death was said to have been the result of idleness forced upon him while the black plague was raging in London. He had the distinction, however, of being the only person to have been honored by an epitaph written by John Milton, or, in fact, by two such epitaphs. Either is too long to be quoted in full, but the second, filled with puns upon his occupation and the cause of his death may be quoted in part:

> *Merely to drive the time away he sickened,*
> *Fainted, and died, nor would with ale be quickened.*
> *"Nay," quoth he, on his swooning bed outstretched,*
> *"If I mayn't carry, sure I'll ne'er be fetched,*
> *But vow, though the cross doctors all stood hearers,*
> *For one carrier put down to make six bearers."*

> *Ease was his chief disease; and to judge right,*
> *He died for heaviness that his cart went light;*
> *His leisure told him that his time was come,*
> *And lack of load made his life burdensome,*
> *That even to his last breath (there be some that say't),*
> *As he were pressed to death, he cried, "More weight."*

Maundy Thursday

The day before Good Friday, the Thursday next before Easter. To most persons not of the Roman Catholic or Episcopalian faiths the designation of this day is incomprehensible, for the term "maundy" now appears in no other connection. It originated from the thirteenth chapter of John, in which the Last Supper and the ceremony and doctrine of humility are described. The thirty-fourth verse, it will be recalled, reads, "A new commandment I give unto you, That ye love one another." The Latin for "a new command-ment" is *mandatum novum*, and these are the words that begin the first antiphon sung after the commemorative observance of the Lord's Supper and the ceremony, in England, of the washing of the feet of a number of poor persons by some member of the royal family or other important person. *Mandatum novum* became early abridged to *mandatum*, and in the common speech of the thirteenth and fourteenth centuries this became further abridged to mandee, monde, maunde, and so on, ultimately becoming maundy. The original commandment itself lost its significance and became applied to the ceremonial washing of feet, except in the observances of some religious denominations.

to get (or *have*) *cold feet*

An American doesn't need to be told that the meaning is to lose one's nerve, to become craven. The slang expression originated during my youth, probably in the early 1890's, but, as has been the case from the earliest times, no one took the trouble to give it a date or to record the exact source. I think it likely that its origin was a literal statement. Some wife, hearing a noise during the night, may have aroused her worthy but timorous husband to investigate the source. He, poor wight, may have said that his feet were too cold—meaning, literally that his feet were so cold and the floor so icy that he couldn't even chase a mouse. "Ya-a-ah," she may have retorted, "you and your cold  feet!" And, if she were like some wives, she lost no time in passing the word around among all his friends that "Ed had such cold feet last night he couldn't even get out of bed for fear a mouse would bite him."

to cotton to (*a thing* or *person*)

We are apt to look upon this as recent, forgetting that it was used by Dickens (*Old Curiosity Shop*) more than a hundred years ago with just the present meaning, to get along with or to like a thing or person. And it was not original with Dickens, for it was used more than thirty years earlier. In fact, the usage appears to be little more than an extension of a meaning that was popular back in the middle of the sixteenth century, in a phrase, now obsolete, "This gear cottons," meaning this matter goes well or prospers. The origin is lost, but probably referred in some manner to the readiness with which cotton adheres to a napped surface.

one-horse town

The "one-horse town" is American; we use the expression disparagingly to designate a town of such limited resources, so sleepy and doless, that one horse might be able to do all its necessary transportation. The usage first reported (1855) credits the expression to New Orleans, but as it was reported a few years later as far north as Boston, a place notably reluctant to accept new terms, it is more than likely that it had come into wide popular use quite a long while before it appeared in print.

kangaroo court

Nowadays, a kangaroo court is rarely heard of except in jails or similar institutions where a mock court, independent of regular legal procedure, is set up by the inmates to try a fellow prisoner for some alleged offense. Sometimes such courts are set up merely for amusement, as diversions against the tedium of imprisonment, and are then nothing but travesties of legal processes. Originally, however, these irregular courts were resorted to in frontier communities, usually for the trial and condemnation of persons committing offenses against the community. The source of the name is mysterious, for it is American rather than Australian; I have not found evidence of its use in Australia at any time. But as the date of origin appears to coincide closely with the gold rush to California in 1849, the guess may be hazarded that the name was in humorous allusion to the early purpose of such courts, to try "jumpers" who, resorting to desperate measures, seized the mining claims of others. As the long arm of government had not yet reached the "diggings," the improvised courts were as irregular as those in today's jails, and perhaps they were sometimes equally unfair.

red-letter day

Such a day may be traced back to the fifteenth century, though in that period the allusion was to a holy day of some sort, such as one memorializing a saint or a church festival. The name came from the custom of using red or purple colors for marking those days upon the calendar, a custom that is still followed generally in showing the dates of Sundays and holy days by red figures on our present calendars. From this ancient custom arose the practice of designating any memorable date as a red-letter day.

not to know (one) from Adam

Wherever this is used the speaker means that he would be wholly unable to recognize the person of whom he speaks, probably a person once known but now forgotten. The source and antiquity are wholly unknown, but it may be that we owe it to the ancient argument over Adam's possession of a navel. Artists, such as Michelangelo, Van Eyck, and Titian, in their paintings of the Creation, always showed both Adam and Eve with navels, but many critics insisted that they could not have possessed them. "Otherwise," we may surmise that they said, "one could not tell ordinary people from Adam!" The argument was used as the basis of the contribution by Dr. Logan Glendenning, in  1944, "The Case of the Missing Patriarchs, to a symposium, *Profile by Gaslight*, which purported to be "the private life of Sherlock Holmes," and which contained fancied episodes about the great detective written by a number of his admirers. Dr. Glendenning recounted an adventure of Holmes after he had died: Consternation reigned in Heaven because Adam and Eve had been missing for several eons. Holmes, whose astuteness was known in Heaven, was assigned to the search. He alone knew all others from Adam and could speedily pick out the missing pair, for he alone of all the myriads who preceded him through the pearly gates knew that they would be the only two without navels.

root hog or die

This means to get down to hard work or suffer the consequences, to shift for oneself. The earliest literary use so far reported goes back only to 1834, to Davy Crockett's autobiography, *A Narrative of the Life of David Crockett*, written just two years before his death at the Alamo. It is likely, however, that this typical Americanism goes back to much earlier pioneering days. It arose, undoubtedly, from the everyday observance of the fact that a hog, if left to forage for himself, is not in much danger of starving. He will root with his snout, or, to use another American term, he will "hog," or appropriate greedily, whatever he can find in the nature of food. It is possible, of course, that the original sense was a command, as it were, to a hog to start rooting or suffer death. But in the use that I have always heard "hog" had merely the force of a verb, one of a triplet, "to root, hog, or die"—just as the phrase, "eat, drink, and be merry."

black Monday

Nowadays, in schoolboy lingo, this is the day after Easter, the day when school is resumed after the Easter holidays. But, although school children may not know it, the day after Easter has been called "black Monday" in England for many centuries as the anniversary of several different tragedies or ominous events. The first was a tragedy, but historical authenticity is uncertain. According to an account written several centuries after the event, on the day after Easter in the year 1209 a large number of English people who had taken residence in Dublin were massacred by the Irish. Five hundred were said to have been slain. Then in 1357, according to an account written in Latin, "the Black Prince," Edward, Prince of Wales, sustained terrific losses in France on the day after Easter because of a great storm. Also, in the year 1360, according to another ancient chronicle, on the fourteenth day of April, or the day after Easter, during the siege of Paris by Edward III, the day was "a ffoule derke day, so bytter colde, that syttyng on horse bak men dyed." Each of these two latter events were said by the respective chroniclers to have been the occasion which gave rise to the term "black Monday"; but be that as it may, the day was actually so called as long ago as the latter part of the fourteenth century.

to rain cats and dogs

When we use this we don't refer to a gentle shower, but to a terrific downpour. Perhaps, because such rain is usually accompanied by heavy thunder and lightning, the allusion was to a cat and dog fight. As far as the records show, this form of the slight exaggeration originated with Jonathan Swift in his *Complete collection of genteel and ingenious conversation*, usually referred to as *Polite Conversation*, written in 1738; but it might have occurred to him to use a politer phrase than was used by a wit eighty-five years earlier who, describing a downpour, said it rained "dogs and polecats."

to show the white feather

To behave in a cowardly manner; to act pusillanimously. The expression comes from the cockpit, the arena or ring where game-cocks are pitted against one another to see which can vanquish the other. Cockfighting is one of the oldest of sports; it is recorded among early Chinese accounts and was practiced in ancient India, Persia, and Egypt. Throughout all this period birds have been selected for fighting abilities and high wagers have been staked between owners, and between friends of each, on the relative prowess of their cocks. But about two centuries ago—at least, no earlier mention has been found—someone made the discovery that if a cock had so  much as one white feather in its tail, that bird was certain to be a poor fighter, that he would run from the other bird and put up no fight at all. Whether this is true or not—and, if true, it seems strange that it was not known hundreds of years earlier—it became fully believed and passed into a byword that, when applied to a person, became a stigma of cowardice.

on the anxious seat (bench)

We use this nowadays to mean in a state of worry or anxiety, but the literal meaning alludes to the "mourners' bench," or seat especially assigned to those of a congregation who, affected by the exhortations of a preacher, have become anxious over their future state and seek repentance. The literal phrase was in use early in the nineteenth century, but the oldest record of the figurative use is in Harriet Beecher Stowe's *The Pearl of Orr's Island*, published in 1862.

to hold water

The literal sense, such as applied to a sound pitcher or bowl, gradually acquired in the early seventeenth century a figurative meaning, as if testing a pitcher for soundness by filling it with water —if unsound, the water would leak out. Thus, figuratively, an unsound argument or fallacious reasoning would not "hold water" if it failed to stand a test.

to acknowledge the corn

This purely American expression means to admit the losing of an argument, especially in regard to a detail; to retract; to admit defeat. It is somewhat over a hundred years old, one account of its origin giving it the date of 1828. In this account, plausible, though unverified, a member of Congress, Andrew Stewart, is said to have stated in a speech that haystacks and cornfields were sent by Indiana, Ohio, and Kentucky to Philadelphia and New York. Charles A. Wickliffe, member from Kentucky, questioned the statement, allowing that haystacks and cornfields could not walk. Stewart then pointed out that he did not mean literal haystacks and cornfields, but the horses, mules, and hogs for which the hay and corn were raised. Wickliffe then rose to his feet, it is said, and drawled, "Mr. Speaker, I acknowledge the corn."

The other account carries no date, but takes us to New Orleans where an upriver countryman is alleged to have fallen among cardsharps. Before the evening was over the farmer had lost not only his purse, but the two barges of produce, one of corn and one of potatoes, which he had brought to market. But in the morning when he went to the river, possibly intending to deny his losses, he found that the barge loaded with corn had sunk during the night and, of course, was now worthless. So when his creditor arrived, demanding that he turn over both potatoes and corn, he said, "I acknowledge the corn, but, by golly, you shan't get the potatoes."

to break the ice

Our present figurative use came, of course, from the maritime necessity of breaking up the ice upon rivers and channels for the navigation of ships and boats in winter. The early extended sense, indicating preparation of a pathway for others, did not arise until late in the sixteenth century—the earliest instance is from the epilog of a curious work written in 1590 by Henry Swinburne, *A briefe Treatise of Testaments and last Willes*: "The author therefore in aduenteuring to breake the yse to make the passage easie for his countrymen, failing sometimes of the fourd, and falling into the pit, may seeme worthie to be pitied." From this metaphorical usage the present sense—to break down a stiff reserve between persons—was slow in developing, or at least was not recorded for another hundred and fifty years.

to walk Spanish

When Jeffie grabs the smaller Johnny by the collar and the seat of the pants, raises him until he must walk on tiptoe and hustles him out of the room, Johnny is "walking Spanish." (Later in life, Johnny may "walk Spanish" by himself by just tip-toeing cautiously out of a place where he may decide he doesn't want to be.) Neither of the youngsters has any notion that their great-great-grandfathers a hundred and twenty-five years ago were saying and doing the same thing. Possibly one could go back another generation or two, but recorded use dates only to 1825. The source is American, and there is little doubt that it alluded originally to the practices attributed to pirates of the Spanish Main in the treatment  of prisoners. Obviously, a captive would be reluctant to "walk the plank" except under compulsion. He might resist even the prod of a knife; but if lifted and partly choked by a powerful buccaneer, the propulsion would be resistless, and, willy-nilly, he would find himself in the sea.

to go scot free

To be exempt from payment, punishment, or penalty. Except in this expression, and in the somewhat rare "to pay one's scot," this meaning of "scot" is almost unknown in America. But it comes straight from Old English; it then meant, as now, a payment, or, especially, one's share in the cost of some entertainment; later it came to mean also a tax. Hence, "to go scot free" is, literally, to be free of payment or tax.

a bolt from the blue

It is a bolt of lightning from the clear, blue sky that is meant. Such a phenomenon is, at least, unexpected and is also startling. Thus the news of the Japanese attack on Pearl Harbor was a bolt from the blue, in the figurative sense. Literary record of the use of the saying dates only to 1888, but it is likely that it existed in common speech many years earlier.

an Achilles' heel

A vulnerable spot. In the *Iliad*, Homer's marvelous legend, Achilles, the hero of the story, was the son of a king, Peleus, and of the sea-goddess, Thetis, and a great-grandson of no less than Zeus himself. The account that Homer gives of the boyhood of so remarkable a being is reasonably prosaic; that is, he was at least brought up on land, even though his tutors did include a centaur. But later writers than Homer felt compelled to provide greater details. Thus, according to one account, the real reason why Achilles was fearless in battle was because he knew that everyone was powerless to hurt him. That was because his mother had dipped him in the river Styx—the river that encircles Hades—and had thus made him invulnerable. He would have been living yet, perhaps, but the god Apollo, who was no friend, knew that Thetis had slipped—she had held Achilles by the heel when she dipped him and had neglected to get that heel wet. Apollo whispered that secret to Paris, mortal enemy of Achilles, who deliberately aimed an arrow at this unprotected heel, the one spot that was vulnerable, and thus caused the death of the hero. (Incidentally, the tendon leading upward from the rear of the heel is even today called "Achilles' tendon.")

to paddle one's own canoe

This was probably used in nothing but its literal sense until the appearance in *Harper's Monthly*, in 1854, of a song by Dr. Edward P. Philpots. Since then, however, it has been more frequently used to mean, to show one's independence. The refrain of the song ran:

> *Voyager upon life's sea:—*
> *To yourself be true,*
> *And whate'er your lot may be,*
> *Paddle your own canoe.*

a dog in the manger

Aesop, back about 600 B.C., is said to have told his master about a dog which went to sleep in a manger full of hay. According to the fable, the ox, for whom the manger had been filled, came up to it for his rations, whereupon the dog, roused from his slumbers, snapped at the ox and drove him away. The ox, annoyed by this behavior, accused the dog of being churlish, because, he said, "You are unable to eat the hay yourself but will not leave it for those who can." Or, in the quaint words of John Gower, in *Confessio Amantis*, written about 1390, "Thogh it be noght the houndes kinde To ete chaf, yit wol he werne (prevent) An oxe which comth to the berne (barn), Therof to taken eny fode."

to set the Thames on fire

It is the English river that is referred to, not Connecticut's. But the saying has been used of other rivers and with the same thought—in Ireland of the Liffey, in the United States of the Hudson, and in Germany of the Rhine. The German saying—*Er hat den Rhein und das Meer angezündet* (He has set the Rhine and the ocean afire)—dating back to about 1580, is of earlier vintage than the English by about two hundred years. In all instances, the figurative meaning is to build up a reputation for oneself, as if by such a miraculous stunt as to set a river afire; to do something wonderful.

A writer in *Notes & Queries*, about eighty years ago, advanced the theory that, perhaps through similarity of pronunciation, the English saying might originally have been, "to set the temse on fire"

—"temse" being an old-fashioned name for the sieve used in bolting meal. Thus, "He will never set the temse on fire," he argued, might have had reference to some extremely slow workman. There is no historical basis for this theory, however.

till the cows come home

Although cows are always milked twice a day, mornings and evenings, this very old homely saying refers to the time that cows, with udders painfully full, come to the home gates for the morning milking. The saying, used as long  ago as 1600, seems at first to have always indicated disgracefully late hours, mostly hours spent riotously; but Swift, in 1738, applied it to time spent by a slugabed who did not arise before the evening milking: "I warrant you lay abed till the cows came home," he wrote in *Polite Conversation.* The amplified expression, "Till hell freezes over and the cows come skating home over the ice," is very modern.

to raise Cain

In the United States, one raises Cain when he causes a disturbance, or, perhaps, when one gets so angry that he loses his temper. The saying is generally believed to refer to the first child of Adam and Eve, Cain, who killed his brother, Abel, through jealousy and whose name has always been synonymous with fratricide. It is not surprising that the first literary use of the expression should have this reference, a witticism in the *St. Louis Pennant* of 1840: "Why have we every reason to believe that Adam and Eve were both rowdies? Because . . . they both raised Cain."

It seems more likely to me, however, that the expression was originally a play upon words. Cain was, it is true, a son of Adam and Eve; but for many centuries and to the present time in Scotland and Ireland, the Gaelic word "cain" or "kain" or "cane" has meant the rent of land, payable in produce. One who "raises cain" is actually raising the produce to pay for his land. Some Scottish or Irish settler in the United States may have used the term literally in all seriousness to a jocular neighbor. There is no evidence supporting the hypothesis, however.

to draw the longbow

The longbow was the type of bow said to have been used by Robin Hood; that is, a bow about the length of a man, as distinguished from the old short bow used at the Battle of Hastings, or from the crossbow. The longbow, as compared with either of the others, was greatly superior in range and in accuracy. Famous archers vied with one another in using the longbow, and great tales were told of their prowess. One archer, according to an old ballad, was so skilled that, in an exhibition before the king, he split a slender wand at a distance of 400 yards (almost a quarter of a mile), then to impress the king still more, he tied his own seven-year-old son to a stake, balanced an apple upon the lad's head, and, from a distance of 120 yards, split the apple.

Great tales were told of the remarkable shots these English bowmen made—and the tales lost nothing in the telling. They became as discredited as the modern fish story. Hence, anyone believed to be telling a fantastic story was said to draw the longbow. Probably the saying came into use long before the seventeenth century, though the first literary record appeared late in that century.

on the horns of a dilemma

A dilemma, in logic, is a form of argument in which a participant finds himself in the embarrassing predicament of having to make a choice of either of two premises, both of which are obnoxious; it is a trap set by an astute person to catch an unwary one, like answering yes or no to the question, "Have you stopped beating your wife?" Because one may be caught and impaled upon either of the alternatives, each of them has been called a "horn." Medieval scholars, writing in Latin, used the expression, *argumentum cornutum*, horned argument. Nicolas Udall, in his translations of the adages collected (in Latin) by Erasmus explains the saying in the language of 1548: "Thys forked questyon; which the sophisters call an horned question, because that to whether of both partyes a bodye shall make a direct aunswere, he shall renne on the sharpe poyncte of the horne."

by hook or by crook

This phrase is so old that it has become a recognized part of the language. It appears in the writings of John Wyclif and of John Gower, both of whom were contemporaries of Chaucer. It meant then, as it does today, "in one way or another; by fair means or foul"; but no one knows why it has that meaning. Attempts to solve the riddle have been numerous; various theories have been advanced and stoutly defended, but none yet has been definitely proved. The most plausible relates to the old forest laws of England, laws by which all forest lands of the country were the private property of the king. The sole right of the common people to enter these forests without permission was, it is said, for the removal of dead wood from the ground or dead branches from the trees; of the latter, only such branches as could be brought down "by hook or by crook," that is, by the use of no stouter instrument than a reaper's hook or a shepherd's crook. But in order to satisfy the meaning, "by fair means or foul," we must assume that some of the ancient shepherds found an excuse to tend their sheep with crooks that were exceedingly long or unusually heavy.

to turn the tables

Metaphorically speaking, we turn the tables upon another fellow when we put him in the predicament that we have been occupying, or into a similar one. There is no connection with "turning the other cheek." The saying arose during the early 1600s, some three centuries ago, and seems to have been applied to some popular card game in which a player, when at a disadvantage, might reverse the position of the board and thus shift the disadvantage to his adversary. Or possibly the original sense of the expression was the same as we now indicate by "duplicate," as in duplicate bridge, that after a series of hands of cards had been played, the table was turned and the same series of hands was replayed, each player hold-ing the hand previously held by an opponent.

Brewer has an interesting theory that the expression is derived from an ancient Roman masculine fad of purchasing costly tables. After such a purchase, the matron of the house, chided for a purchase of her own, was alleged to "turn the tables" by reminding her spouse of his extravagance. Marital customs of Roman days were not unlike the present, so it is not unlikely that the matrons did thus defend themselves, but evidence is lacking that our meta-phor had such an origin.

to keep the pot boiling

Even among the ancients the container often signified the thing contained; the Romans used *olla*, pot, many times instead of the meat within the pot, and so did our own forbears. Hence, when they said that they must keep the pot boiling, they meant that they must have something within the pot, which, when removed, would be edible; that is, that they must supply meat or other material for a stew, provide a livelihood. This was the only figurative meaning from the sixteenth to the nineteenth century; it gave rise to such allied sayings as "to go to pot" (to cut up and prepare for the pot; hence, in present usage, to become disintegrated), "potboiling," (doing something, usually something of no great merit, that will provide for one's immediate needs).

at (or on) first blush

Anciently, a blush was a glimpse, a momentary view. This was the sense that we find in the late fourteenth-century poem, "Joseph of Arithmathie": "Aftur the furste blusch we ne michte him biholden (After the first glimpse we could not behold him)." This sense dropped out of use during the sixteenth century, however, except in the present phrase.

to carry coals to Newcastle

The current American equivalent is "to sell refrigerators to the Eskimos." The idea is of doing something that is the height of superfluity. In explanation, Newcastle—or Newcastle upon Tyne, to use the official name of this ancient English city—lies in the center of the great coal-mining region of England. Vast quantities of coal are shipped out of it by rail and by sea every day. Hence, he would be a fool indeed who brought coal from another region into the place where it was naturally so plentiful. The saying was recorded by Heywood in 1606; as he labeled it common even then, it may well go back a century or two earlier. Similar sayings occur in all languages.

to talk turkey

A century ago, it would seem, the turkey was considered a pleasant bird, for when such expressions as "to talk turkey" or "to say turkey" were used, the allusion was to a pleasant conversation. A young man "talked turkey" to a good-looking girl, if he had the chance. Perhaps that was because a young man in the presence of a

pretty girl gets so tongue-tied that his remarks sound as meaningless as the gobble of a turkey. But sometime within the past fifty or sixty years the gobble of the turkey acquired a sterner note; it began to have the qualities of the voice of a father berating his son for the dent in the fender of the family car, or that of the employer who, in no uncertain tones, jumps down the throat of a clerk for a heedless error.

There is a legend, variously reported, that is often used in explanation of the way this expression arose: Two men, one an Indian, went for a day's hunting. They shot several birds, among them one or more turkeys; but when it came time to divide the bag, the smart white man, thinking to take advantage of an ignorant savage, always arranged the counting in such way that the turkeys fell to his share. The Indian, however, was not so gullible as he seemed. Finally he faced his companion. "Ugh," he said, "All time you talk turkey. Now I talk turkey to you."

in hot water

Perhaps because hot water is so easily obtainable these days, we think of the figurative hot water, meaning a trouble, a scrape, or a difficulty, as being a modern expression. No, indeed! People first got into trouble thousands of years ago, though English-speaking people didn't refer to it as "hot water" until about the beginning of the sixteenth century. Possibly the allusion was to the ancient way that unwelcome guests were sometimes warded off—by heaving a kettleful of boiling water, when available, upon troublesome intruders. But, oddly enough, more than two centuries after the figurative use was a matter of record, James Harris, before starting on the great diplomatic career that eventually caused him to be created Earl of Malmesbury, supposed that "in hot water" was a modern phrase of his period, and called it such, in 1765, in one of his letters.

to eat humble pie

This, meaning to humble oneself, to apologize or abase oneself profoundly, was originally a play upon words, a jocular substitution of humble for umble wherein the meaning of humble was retained. Umble pie was, and maybe still is in some parts of England, a pasty made of the edible inward parts of an animal, usually a deer. The umbles were considered a delicacy by most persons, although some thought them to be fit only for menials. And the pie made of those parts was also variously appreciated; it graced some tables, but James Russell Lowell, in 1864, said, "Disguise it as you will, flavor it as you will, call it what you will, umble-pie is umble-pie, and nothing else."

Etymologically the phrase is interesting; though in present use it is humble pie, jocularly derived from umble pie, umble is one of a number of English words which originally had an initial "n." Thus, just as apron was originally napron, adder (the snake) originally nadder, so umble was originally numble. But there would have been no point to the joke then, without an initial vowel to which cockney "h" might be prefixed.

to haul (rake, bring, or fetch) over the coals

Until comparatively recent times the sin of heresy was, in many countries, punishable by death. In England, during the fifteenth and sixteenth centuries, one found guilty of departing from the creed and tenets of the church might be condemned to death by burning. Thus, the earliest uses of this expression, back in the sixteenth century, referred to the literal punishment of heretics—one would be fetched over the coals literally unless he speedily reformed his actions and beliefs. From the use of the expression as a threat, almost at once it became a synonym for the sense in which we use it today—to reprimand severely, to censure caustically.

wet blanket

This, one might have supposed, is certainly an example of recent American slang, but it was used in Scotland more than a hundred years ago, and with exactly the meaning in which we use it today—one who puts a damper on anything, especially upon any jollity; one who emits gloom. The expression was used in 1830 by the Scottish novelist, John Galt, in Lawrie Todd, or the Settlers in the Woods: "I have never felt such a wet blanket before or syne." But as this novel contains sketches of American frontier life, the author creates an illusion of American slang.

to sweat blood

To perform such arduous toil or to be in such physical agony that the sweat in which one is bathed seems to be one's blood draining away. The allusion is to the agony of Jesus on the Mount of Olives: "And being in an agony he prayed more earnestly: and his sweat was as it were great drops of blood falling down to the ground." The expression had only a religious use until about the seventeenth century.

a big shot

A person of importance. This slang use is quite recent, developed within the current century, but it is a lineal descendant of "a big gun," dating from the middle of the last century, and which in turn sprang from the union of "a great gun" and "a big bug" of the early nineteenth century.

the lion's share

Why this always means the greater part in any allotment, especially the part that one gives to the "boss" or that, in serving the dessert, mother apportions to father, takes us back to one of Aesop's fables. Two versions have come down to us, which is not surprising, for old Aesop is supposed merely to have told his fables, leaving it to others to write them out in later centuries.

In one of these, a lion, an ass, and a fox went hunting, with the understanding that the prey should be divided among them. A large fat stag was caught, and the ass was appointed to divide it. This he did with scrupulous exactitude, apportioning an equal amount, as best he could, to each of them. But this enraged the lion, who felt that his  size, prowess, and dignity had been insulted. He was so infuriated that he flew at the ass and killed him. Then the fox undertook to divide the stag into proper portions; and, being crafty and not wishing to follow the fate of the ass, he nibbled off a small piece for himself and left all the rest to the lion.

In the other version, there were four hunters, a lion, a heifer, a goat, and a sheep. Again the prey was a large fat stag, but in this story the lion did the dividing. He divided it neatly enough into four equal portions, taking the tastiest part for himself. But, having done so, he took another portion, saying that it was his by right of being the strongest. A third portion followed, because, he said, it was his by right of being the most valiant. The fourth portion belonged, he said, to the others—and then he added, "But touch it if you dare!"

to get the bird

Actors get the bird when the performance is so bad that the audience rebels, by hissing or booing, or, in more recent years, by executing the Bronx cheer. The expression was the forerunner of getting the raspberry. It dates from about the middle of the nineteenth century, being first recorded in Hotten's *Dictionary of Modern Slang* in 1859. But, in turn, this expression was preceded by its logical forerunner, "to get the goose," in allusion to the hissing of the goose, a theatrical phrase that goes back at least to the beginning of the nineteenth century.

between the devil and the deep sea

On the horns of a dilemma; between Scylla and Charybdis; facing equally perilous dangers. William Walker, in 1670, when compiling his *Phraseologia Anglo-Latina; or Phrases of the English and Latin Tongue*, included this expression in his list, probably finding it used by some earlier writer of Latin; but if so, his source is no longer known. The phrase is listed, however, by James Kelly, in 1721, in his *Complete Collection of Scotish Proverbs*. The view that it is of Scottish origin is supported by the fact that it is to be found in the account written by Colonel Robert Monro, a doughty Scot, *His Expedition with the worthy Scots Regiment called Mac-Keyes Regiment*, relating to his service under Gustavus Adolphus of Sweden between 1621 and 1632. Monro described one engagement, in which he found himself exposed not only to the fire of the enemy, but also to Swedish guns that were not sufficiently elevated, and said, "I, with my partie, did lie on our poste, as betwixt the devill and the deep sea." This is the earliest English use of the phrase that has yet been found.

to blow hot and cold

To be inconsistent; to vacillate. We are indebted to one of Aesop's fables for this meaning. A satyr, he tells us, came upon a traveler in the winter who was blowing upon his fingers. "Why do you do that?" asked the satyr. "To warm my fingers," replied the traveler, "they are nearly frozen." The satyr led the man to his cave where he poured out a mess of hot pottage and laid it before his guest. Thereupon the traveler began to blow the smoking dish with all his might. "What! Is it not hot enough?" cried the satyr. "Indeed, yes," answered the man, "I am trying to cool it." "Away with you," said the alarmed satyr, thrusting the man out of the cave, "I will have no dealings with one who can blow hot and cold from the same mouth."

to know the ropes

To be familiar with all the details. There have been differences of opinion about the origin of this saying, for it so happens that the earliest records make it appear that the phrase was first used by the gentry of the racetracks, and, be-  cause of that, some hold that by "ropes" the allusion is to the reins of a horse's harness; that one "knows the ropes" who best knows the handling of the reins. But, as with many other phrases, this one, I think, undoubtedly originated among sailors. An experienced sailor, in the days of sailing vessels, was one who was familiar with the bewildering array of ropes leading to all parts of the many sheets of canvas under which the vessel sailed. Such a man literally "knew the ropes."

to split hairs

In these days, one engaged in the occupation of splitting hairs might very likely be engaged in some profound scientific work— trying, perhaps, to find some microscopic cause for the dividing of long hair at the ends. But three hundred years ago when the phrase was coined there was no thought of scientific research; it meant to divide into exactly even amounts, so precisely as to afford no slightest advantage. A hundred years later, however, it became an ironic figure of speech; one who would split hairs was one who would argue endlessly over fine distinctions, over differences of trivial im- portance, and this is the sense still in use.

all beer and skittles

The phrase occurs more generally in British literature than in American. Dickens used it (with "porter" instead of "beer") in *Pickwick Papers*, in the scene in which Mr. Pickwick, convicted of breach of promise, is introduced to Fleet Prison as a debtor. His conductor has shown him that other debtors manage to have a pretty good time. "It strikes me, Sam," said Mr. Pickwick to his faithful Achates, Sam Weller, "that imprisonment for debt is scarcely any punishment at all." "Ah, that's just the wery thing, sir," rejoined Sam, "they don't mind it; it's a regular holiday to them—all porter and skittles."

Skittles was a game quite similar to ninepins; so "porter and skittles" or "beer and skittles" was equivalent to a very pleasant occasion, a time of feasting and playing. The expression occurs generally in the negative, as, "life is not all beer and skittles"; i.e., life is not an unmixed pleasure.

best bib and tucker

One's best clothes. The expression as a whole dates from the late eighteenth century. The bib was an article of attire similar to that worn by children then and now, but also formerly worn by girls and women, and extending from the throat to the waist. The tucker, to quote a historian of 1688, was "a narrow piece of Cloth which compasseth the top of a Womans Gown about the Neck part"; it was often a frill of lace over the shoulders. Men whose calling required an apron, such as mechanics or drovers, sometimes wore a bib; no man ever wore a tucker. The expression, therefore, was originally never applied to a man, but when the literal meaning of the words became dimmed, either a man or a woman was said to don his best bib and tucker when he dressed up for some momentous occasion.

to steer (or sail) between Scylla and Charybdis

To steer a mid-course between perils. Scylla, according to Homer's *Odyssey*, was a fearful monster that dwelt in a cavern on the face of a high cliff that overlooked a narrow channel of the sea. She had six heads, each on a long neck, and from every ship that passed each mouth seized a sailor. On the opposite rock grew a wild fig tree, beneath which Charybdis, three times a day, sucked in and regorged the sea. It was the fate of Odysseus (or, in Latin, Ulysses) to sail between these two perils, to try to avoid the loss of his crew from the monster and the loss of his ship in the whirlpool at the base of the opposite rock. Odysseus lost both his crew and his ship, saving his own life by clinging to the fig tree.

to curry favor

"Fauvel" was the name of a fallow-colored horse, in the fourteenth-century allegory, *Roman de Fauvel*, a horse used to symbolize fraud and cunning. The allegory achieved great popularity in France as well as in England. Perhaps in ironic jest, a person who indulged in fulsome flattery was said "to curry Fauvel," meaning that he sought by fraud and cunning to gain the good will of the person he flattered. This, in the English spelling of that day became corrupted into "to curry Favel," and a toady or sycophant became known as a "curry-favel." Popular speech took up the phrase, but the popular ear did not hear it quite correctly; so *favel*  became *favor* several hundred years ago, and gave us an expression, "to curry favor," that had no literal meaning, but which was used then, as now, to mean to flatter subtly in order to gain some end. In French, many years ago, they made a verb of "Fauvel"—*faufiler* —which has the meaning of our entire phrase.

to lead apes in hell

This expression was common in the times of Shakespeare and is found in *The Taming of the Shrew* in the lines where Katharina says to her father, "Nay, now I see she is your treasure, she must have a husband; I must dance bare-foot on her wedding day and for your love to her lead apes in hell." Beatrice uses the same expression in *Much Ado about Nothing*. Another writer of the same period gives us the meaning in the lines, " 'Tis an old proverb, and you know it well, that women dying maids lead apes in hell." But why spinsters were ever consigned to such an ignoble fate after death, and what was the source or the age of the proverb, were probably unknown even in Shakespeare's days.

to spill the beans

To upset the plans; to relate something fully or prematurely; to let the cat out of the bag; to upset the apple cart. This American saying came into general use early in the present century, and, of course, the incident that gave rise to it, whatever it may have been, was not recorded. Very likely it was an actual occurrence, possibly an important occasion at which, say, baked beans were to have been the main dish. Just before serving, or perhaps at the table, the bean pot may have broken, not only causing a mess generally, but also upsetting the plans. The extended sense, telling something that should not be told, or telling something in detail, seems to have been added from the older, "to know beans," to know what is what.

to walk the chalk

In present-day American use, one who is made "to walk the chalk" must walk a line of rectitude and sobriety, not deviating a hair's breadth, or he must obey the rules closely. The significance is alleged to have been of nautical origin, a straight chalk line drawn along the deck, or a narrow lane between two lines, to test the

sobriety of a sailor; if he could not walk the length of the line placing each foot directly on it, or if he was unable to keep within the two lines of the lane, he was adjudged to be too drunk for duty and was clapped into the brig. By the time the expression had become a matter of literary record, back in 1823, however, the test was military and altogether a friendly competition among soldiers to discover who was the most sober. The British say that the original test was a custom in the American navy, but the Dictionary of American English has no record of it.

Both in England and America, however, there was another meaning of "to walk the chalk (or chalks)." It is now obsolete in America, but its meaning was to take one's speedy departure. Mark Twain used it in Sketches, New and Old, "If anybody come meddlin' wid you, you jist make 'em walk chalk." This usage is recorded in England as early as 1842, though the original allusion cannot be ascertained.

to turn turtle

One must remember that "turtle" applies, scientifically speaking, to the marine member of the family, and that "tortoise" should properly be used to describe the land or fresh-water member. The sea beastie is the one most highly prized for food, nowadays chiefly appearing on the menu as "turtle soup." Our English-speaking ancestors, however, called both the land and sea species "tortoises" until the middle of the seventeenth century, for it was not until then that they began to realize that the huge marine creature, unknown to them before the travels of Columbus, Cabot, and other explorers, was not just an overgrown land specimen. Sailors started to speak of this animal as a "turtle," probably thinking that they were giving it the French name, *tortue*, though in reality they were giving to this quadruped a name that had previously been applied only to the bird which we now call "turtle dove."

Also some time in the seventeenth century, sailors found that these sea monsters were edible, if one could first capture them. Caribbean natives, they observed, waited until one of the reptiles came ashore to lay her eggs, then, seizing her by one of her flippers, turned her over on her back. Thus careened, she was absolutely helpless. This the sailors called "turning the turtle." Later, because a ship that had been capsized bore a fancied resemblance to an overturned turtle, sailors called such capsizing, "turning the turtle." Ashore, that saying was adopted for anything that was upside down.

to bark up the wrong tree

To mistake one's course of action; to be on the wrong course; to have one's attention diverted from the intended object. Literally, this American phrase referred to a hunting dog used in the pursuit of raccoons. When this nocturnal animal takes to a tree, the dog is supposed to stay at the foot of the tree and bay until its master arrives. But, in the dark, if the dog mistakes the tree in which the 'coon has taken refuge, the hunter may lose it entirely. The expression must have been very popular in the early nineteenth century, especially by writers of western life and tales, for in rapid succession it appeared in the works of James Hall, David Crockett, and Albert Pike.

to hold the bag

When one is left holding the bag he is being made the scapegoat, he has been left in an awkward predicament not of his own devising, or blamed for or punished for all the faults committed jointly by himself and others. George Washington may have been familiar with the saying during the Revolutionary War, for it was used by an

American army officer, Major Royall Tyler, in literature for the first time, when, in 1787, he wrote the first comedy to be written and produced in America. This young officer had participated in the suppression of Shays's Rebellion in the previous year and, in his play, has one of his characters say, "General Shays has sneaked off and given us the bag to hold."

There was a much earlier expression, dating back to the sixteenth century, "to give the bag," which meant to give one the slip, to elude someone, and also, to abandon. It is likely that the bag that was given was the same bag as that which one was left holding. Neither the bag of the sixteenth century nor its contents, if any, is identified, but as the saying was used in speaking of a servant or apprentice who left without notification, it is highly probable that the original bag was empty, that the servant had absconded with his master's cash, leaving him only an empty purse.

to jump out of the frying pan into the fire

The same expression or one closely allied to it is common to many languages; in the second century the Greek equivalent was "out of the smoke into the flame"; the Italian and Portuguese, "to fall from the frying pan into the coals"; the Gaelic, "out of the cauldron into the fire," and the French, from which the English may be a translation, "to leap from the frying pan into the fire (*tomber de la poêle dans le feu*)." The sense of the expression has always been to escape one evil predicament by leaping into another just as bad or worse.

English usage is traceable to a religious argument that arose between William Tyndale, translator of the Bible into English, and Sir Thomas More, best remembered now as the author of Utopia. The argument started in 1528 upon the publication of a paper by More, *A Dialoge concerning Heresyes*. This elicited a treatise from Tyndale in 1530, *An Answere unto Sir Thomas Mores Dialoge*, and this in turn brought forth from More, two years later, *The Confutacyon of Tyndales Answere*, wherein More brings in our expression, saying that his adversary "featly conuayed himself out of the frying panne fayre into the fyre." It is a little grim to recall that Tyndale was publicly strangled and burned as a heretic in 1536, but that More was not alive to rejoice, for he, a year earlier, had been hung, through perjured testimony, as a traitor because he would not approve the bigamous marriage of Henry VIII to Anne Boleyn.

the apple of one's eye

Literally this is the pupil of the eye. In ancient times it was called an apple because it was thought to be a solid globular body. But even by the time of King Alfred—that is, in the ninth century—because injury to the pupil would render one blind, the expression had come to mean that which one holds dearest.

to be caught flat-footed

Unlike "flat-footed" in the phrase, "to come out flat-footed," one is caught flat-footed when undecided or unprepared. It is likely that the term came from the American game of football, for it applies most pertinently to the player who, having received the ball on a pass, is caught by an opposing player before he has moved from his tracks.

within an ace of

About as close as possible; on the very edge of. At dice, an ace is the lowest number, and ambsace—literally, both aces, from the Old French, *ambes as*—is the lowest possible throw, hence the epitome of bad luck, almost nothing. Thus, "ambsace" very naturally came to mean an extremely small point; less of a point than would be represented by the pip of a single ace. And, in the same figurative manner, "within ambsace of" measured a degree of closeness that was no more than half a pip or jot. This latter wording appears to have been the original form of the expression; but, through careless use or faulty hearing, this became corrupted into the only form heard today, "within an ace of," though both wordings were in use in the seventeenth century.

to fly the coop

This is American slang, apparently twentieth century, though it is likely that it was criminal cant originally and may date back to  the nineteenth century. "Coop" is slang for prison, jail; the original meaning was, therefore, to escape from prison. By later extension the phrase has come to mean to depart unceremoniously from any place, especially from a place that has begun to feel confining or restrictive. Thus a boy at school tells his fellows that he is going "to fly the coop," when he intends to "play hooky"; that is, to leave the school grounds without permission. Or, humorously, one at a party that he does not enjoy, is said "to have flown the coop" if he has left without formal leave-taking.

Attic salt

This has nothing to do with anything that may be found in one's attic, but refers rather to Attica, the ancient kingdom and republic of Greece. The people of this country, especially of its capital, Athens, were noted for the delicacy and refinement of their wit. It was so nobably piquant or salty that even in Rome it was described as *sal Atticum*, of which our phrase, "Attic salt," is merely the translation.

through thick and thin

Through evil times and good; through foul weather and fair; steadfastly. The expression may be traced back to Chauncer's *The Reeves Tale* where, in the escapade of the clerk's horse, we read:

And whan the hors was loos, he gan to goon
Toward the fen ther wilde mares renne,
Forth with "wi-he!" thurgh thikke and eek thurgh thenne.

But Spenser, in *The Faerie Queene*, supplies the best clue to the probable original meaning in the lines:

His tyreling Jade he fiersely forth did push
Through thicke and thin, both over banck and bush.

That is, if the rider was pushing his steed over a straight course and over "banck and bush," he was also likely to be going through both thickets and thin woods; and this, it is thought, was the original expression, so old that it had been contracted even before the time of Chaucer.

a fidus Achates

A faithful Achates; a steadfast friend. The saying comes from Virgil's *Aeneid* where Achates is described as the friend who accompanied Aeneas on all his wanderings.

Jim Crow

You can read about Thomas D. Rice in the encyclopedia. He was a comedian of a hundred years ago, turning to Negro minstrelsy almost at the outset of his theatrical career and rapidly attaining especial eminence in this field. He introduced a number of popular songs of that period—one especially, about 1835, with the title "Jim Crow," that became extremely popular. The first verse and chorus of this song, which was accompanied with an appropriate dance step, ran:

Come, listen all you gals and boys,
I'se just from Tucky hoe;
I'm goin' to sing a little song,
My name's Jim Crow.

Chorus *Wheel about and turn about and do jis' so;*
Ebery time I wheel about I jump Jim Crow.

It cannot be stated positively that "Jim Crow," as an appellation of a Negro, arose from this song or that the appellation was of earlier date. No earlier record exists, yet across the ocean, in London, a book against slavery, with the title *The History of Jim Crow*, came out just a few years after the song was first heard. And, not long ago, The Negro Year Book for 1925 recorded the career of a Negro slave of the early nineteenth century, one Jim Crow, born in Richmond, who, eventually freed by his master, went to London and amassed a considerable fortune.

to have one's heart in one's shoes

This is no more than the current version of a very old saying that describes extreme fear. An ancient humorist, wishing to imply that his heart sank lower with fear than another's could, wrote, in the early fifteenth century, that his heart fell down into his toe. Successively through the centuries, and depending somewhat upon the costume of the period, the heart has metaphorically sunk to one's heel, to one's hose, to one's boots.

to play second fiddle (or violin)

In order to produce the harmony desired by the composer of an orchestral piece, someone must be willing to play the violin of lower tone, or second violin, while another plays the first violin and the leading part. Hence, metaphorically, we speak of anyone who occupies a subordinate position, especially of a person who steps from a leading position into the lesser status, as one who plays second fiddle. And we use the expression also to describe a suitor who, though still smiled upon by the girl of his heart, is not her favorite but is her second choice should the first fail her. Both the academic "violin" and the colloquial "fiddle" have been used in the expression for some two centuries or more, but the latter is more common in America.

amen corner

Who started it and just when is not on the record, but there is little doubt that the "amen corner" was familiar in some American churches, probably Methodist, early in colonial history. Some little church, very likely, began it by placing a bench for the deacons in a corner up toward the front of the congregation, perhaps so that they might the better see who was not paying attention to the sermon. These deacons or other saints, perhaps to keep awake themselves or perhaps merely to show how closely they were following the preacher's discourse, began to express approval audibly, instead of just nodding the head, whenever he said something particularly fitting. This was done by saying "amen," perhaps quietly or perhaps with great enthusiasm and unction when aroused by the dramatic fervor of some portion of the sermon. The original experiment was undoubtedly a success because the practice spread to other churches. This special seat was originally called the "deacons' bench"—a term later applied to a settee in front of a fireplace—but, though not in print before 1868, the disrespectful and popular name given to it was the "amen corner."

Many years later, toward the end of the nineteenth century, the newspapers of New York City began to call a room of the Fifth Avenue Hotel, reserved especially for the group of politicians currently in power, the "amen corner," possibly because the last word in regard to city politics was said there.

Of independent formation, a street corner in London, no longer in existence, was anciently known as the Amen Corner. It was so called because, on Corpus Christi Day, the monks proceeding to St. Paul's Cathedral, singing the *Pater Noster* (thus giving the name "Paternoster Row" to the street they traversed), reached the turn of the road as they sang the *Amen*.

once in a blue moon

It means extremely infrequently, so rarely as to be almost tantamount to never. From literary evidence the unusual tinge to the face of the moon which led someone to call it a "blue moon" was not observed until after the middle of the last century; nevertheless it is highly probable that this phenomenon had been observed by mariners some centuries earlier, but, like many other notions and expressions long familiar to seafaring men, it did not come to the notice of writers for many, many years. But, with another thought in mind, as long ago as 1528 a rimester published these lines:

Yf they saye the mone is belewe,
We must beleve that it is true.

Then the next year "green cheese" entered the picture in the lines of another writer: "They woulde make men beleue . . . that ye Moone is made of grene cheese."

Apparently, then, there were two schools of thought back in the early sixteenth century—one maintaining that "ye Moone" was made of "grene" cheese, and the other stoutly affirming that it was "belewe." Actually these ancient humorists were just punsters with a taste for metaphor; for by "green cheese," it was not the color but the freshness that was referred to—the moon, when full and just rising, resembling both in color and shape a newly pressed cheese. By "blue cheese" the ancient reference was to a cheese that had become blue with mold, metaphorically transferred, probably, to the comparatively rare appearance of the moon on unusually clear nights when the entire surface of the moon is visible although no more than a thin edge is illuminated. Thus, our phrase, "once in a blue moon" may actually date back to the sixteenth-century saying that "the mone is belewe."

none of one's funeral

The explanation of this American saying appears in the first printed account of its use. This was in the Oregon *Weekly Times* in 1854: "A boy said to an outsider who was making a great ado during some impressive mortuary ceremonies, 'What are you crying about? It's none of your funeral.' " The boy meant, of course, that the funeral was of no concern to the bystander. I have no doubt, however, that the boy quoted by the Oregon paper was merely using an expression that was already long current, at least in the West. It traveled widely and may have been taken east by returning forty-niners or others, for within the next two decades it appeared in many eastern sections of the country and was heard even on the floor of Congress.

to pull wires (or *strings*)

A wirepuller these days is one who uses political influence or the like to gain some end or to win an advantage. We in the United States have known such people for the past hundred years. But the original wirepuller was the artist in a marionette show who manipulated the strings or wires that moved the limbs of the puppets.

to cast sheep's eyes at

"To kesten kang eien upon yunge wummen," was the Old English way of expressing the same thought. In modern words, that would read, "to cast wanton eyes upon young women," to gaze upon them amorously. John Skelton, who was decidedly a humorous versifier of the early sixteen century, softened those amorous looks of the young swains of his day by endowing upon them the soft, tender eyes of the sheep, for to him is credited the first use of "casting sheep's eyes" at the fair women of his day. His namesake and fellow humorist of our day, "Red" Skelton, might say, "Oh yeah! Sheep's eyes in wolves' clothing!"

swan song

In ancient times, back when it was thought that a crocodile wept after eating a man, it was also the belief that a swan, unable all its life to sing like other birds, would burst forth into glorious song when it felt the approach of death. According to Plato, Socrates explained the song as one of gladness because the swan, sacred to Apollo, was shortly to be able to join the god it served. As Apollo was the god of poetry and song, it was also the belief that the souls of a poet passed after death into the body of a swan. These ancient beliefs may .be traced through all European literature; in England, we find them in Chaucer, Shakespeare, Byron, and many other writers. From this picturesque source we owe the allusion to the last work of any poet, writer, or orator as his "swan song," supposedly the culmination of all his artistry, his finest work.

to go off half-cocked

This is what we say in America; the British equivalent is "to go off half-cock" or "at half-cock." Either way the meaning is to speak or do something hastily, without adequate preparation, prematurely. The original reference, back in the middle of the eighteenth century, was to the musket which, if the hammer was cocked halfway, was  supposed to be locked, safe against accidental discharge. But sometimes the mechanism was faulty, the hammer would be released, and the gun would be prematurely discharged, with the musketeer wholly unprepared. The thought has been expressed that the allusion is to what happens when a hunter, excited upon seeing his quarry, attempts to shoot his gun without releasing the trigger from the safety position while it is still half-cocked; hence, that he was unprepared. But such reasoning seems faulty, for, as nothing would happen, the gun could not be said to "go off."

to come out flat-footed

There are no ans, ifs, nor buts in the statement of one who "comes out flat-footed"; you know exactly what he means and where he stands. We picture him as planted firmly on both feet, with an air of defiance, daring one to try to shake him from his opinion. The expression originated in the United States; the earliest record of its use yet found is 1846, though "flat-footed" alone, in the sense of determined, positive, is found some twenty years earlier.

not a Chinaman's chance

Having no chance at all; afforded no opportunity whatever. In the early days of the California gold rush something over forty thousand Chinese came into the United States, most of them staying in California. They were not popular in the gold camps, for they were willing to work for almost nothing and, unable to speak the language, were despised by the Americans. Human life was held none too highly in the lawless camps, and a Chinese, friendless and alone, ignorant of American ways, was fair sport for anyone. He had no rights that were respected; even self-defense was not accepted, in a miner's court, against any injury he might commit against another. His chance of survival against any charge was negligible.

proud as (or pleased as) Punch

"Punch" is the chief character, the hump-backed clown, in the comic puppet show, Punch and Judy. The dialog differs, probably, with every showman, but invariably "Punch" is a pompous vainglorious character who in the end lords it magnificently over his shrewish wife, "Judy," and is conspicuously pleased or proud over his ultimate victory, thus giving rise to our present expression.

Probably there are now few children in America or in England who have ever seen a "Punch and Judy Show," but before the days of the "movies" these puppet shows were very popular, exhibited at every old-time county fair. The show originated in Naples about 1600, and is attributed to a comedian, Silvio Fiorillo. In the Italian play, the name of the chief character was Pulcinello; when the show came to England, that name became Punchinello, later contracted to Punch. The British humorous weekly, *Punch*, founded in 1841, owes its name to this old comic show and still carries a figure of the old clown on its masthead.

upside down

Strangely enough, we have had this expression only since the time of Queen Elizabeth. Before that, when one wanted to say that a thing was overturned or in a state of disorder, he said it was "upsedown," or, with the same meaning, "topsy-turvy." From a variety of evidence, the early form of *upsedown* was *up so down*, but nothing has yet been found that would explain this Old English usage, nor, indeed, explain the source of "topsy-turvy."

to keep the ball rolling

The host or hostess, if properly conforming with the precepts of Emily Post, "keeps the ball rolling" at a dinner-party or other occasion by maintaining conversation or relating some anecdote or by providing other entertainment that will keep the interest of the guests from flagging. The saying is of British origin, dating back to the eighteenth century, and alludes either to the game of Rugby or to the game of bandy, probably the latter. Bandy, which is called hockey in America, dates back at least to the sixteenth century, but the puck is a small ball, even when the game is played on the ice. Needless to say, either in this game or in Rugby, if the ball is not in motion interest in the game has certainly flagged.

greasy luck

To a Nantucketer, this is just a way of saying "good luck!" It is a hang-over from the days of whaling, and meant that the well-wisher hoped that the whaleman would quickly fill his ship with oil.

to knuckle under (or down)

Nowadays we usually think of the knuckles as the joints of the fingers, but there was a time when the knuckle meant the knee or the elbow, especially the rounded part of the bone when the joint is bent. This sense survives chiefly in allusion to a joint of meat and in certain phrases. Thus, "to knuckle under," meaning to submit to—

or acknowledge oneself defeated by —another, carries back to the time when one knelt before one's conqueror in token of submission, put the knuckles of one's knees to the ground. Some writers use "to knuckle down," with the same implication.

"To knuckle down to" carries a different significance. It arises from the early inclusion of the bones of the spinal column as "knuckles" also. Hence, one knuckles down to work when he puts his back into it, when he applies himself diligently to it.

Of course, as any small boy knows, one "knuckles down" in the game of marbles; he gets the knuckles of his fingers on the ground, if an adversary insists, so that when he is ready to shoot, his marble will be directly above the spot where it had come to rest, not "fudged" a few inches closer to an opposing marble.

to play ducks and drakes

To squander foolishly or carelessly. The allusion is to the ancient pastime of skipping stones over the water, in some places called "playing ducks and drakes" because the stones, skimming over the surface, are supposed to resemble water fowl rising from a pond. Many stones, thrown even by an expert, fail to skip, and all eventually lose momentum and are lost beneath the water. So, a person who takes his patrimony and spends it carelessly, getting only a brief enjoyment from it, has been said to play ducks and drakes with his money. The figurative allusion dates from the beginning of the seventeenth century; the game was described, in 1585, by John Higgins in *The Nomenclator, or Remembrancer of Adrianus Junius:* "A kind of sport or play with an oister shell or stone throwne into the water, and making circles yer it sinke. . . . It is called a ducke and a drake, and a halfe-penie cake."

to see which way the cat jumps

We use this in a figurative sense as meaning to notice how events are shaping (so as to be able to act accordingly). It is the general assumption that the saying came from the game of tipcat, which boys have been playing since the sixteenth century at least. In this game the "cat" is a short stick of wood, about an inch and a half or so in diameter and five or six inches long, each end tapered from the center like the frustum of a cone. In playing the game the "cat" is struck on one of its tapered ends with sufficient force to cause it to spring into the air and is then knocked away by the player. To strike the "cat" while in the air the player must observe closely the direction of its spring.

But figurative expressions do not often arise from boys' games; they are more likely to achieve permanence from the sports of men. For this reason it seems to me that the source of the expression is more likely to have been the same ancient sport which produced the expressions, "room to swing a cat," and "to let the old cat die." That is, the "cat" in this instance was probably tied within a leather sack which in turn, hung from a tree, was used as a target in archery. The sportsman had literally to watch how the cat jumped in order to be able to hit the target.

to pour oil on troubled waters

It was known to both Pliny and Plutarch, in the first century A.D., that oil poured upon a stormy sea would quiet the waves. Five centuries later, according to the Venerable Bede, Bishop Aidan, an

Irish monk of Iona, also knew this "miracle," for after foretelling that a storm would arise, he gave the seamen of a certain vessel some  holy oil and advised them to pour it upon the water to calm the sea and permit the vessel to ride through the storm. But, perhaps because oil was not plentiful, this knowledge seems either to have been lost or to have remained a scientific fact, for we do not find it again referred to until Benjamin Franklin, in 1774, refers to Pliny's statement in some correspondence. But when whale fishing became a great industry, beginning toward the end of the eighteenth century, and oil in large quantities was available, especially on whaling vessels, it is likely that the scientific phenomenon was often made use of. By the middle of the nineteenth century, at least, the fact was so well known that the expression began to be used metaphorically. Oil poured on troubled waters, as we use it today, means something offered for easing a troubled condition.

blood, toil, tears, and sweat

Winston Churchill had just been appointed prime minister. The war against Germany had been going badly; an attempt to overcome the German invasion of Norway had met with severe losses, and British morale was at low ebb in the spring of 1940. The populace and Parliament hoped for miracles, but Churchill wanted them to know that grim reality faced them and that they must throw off their lethargy. "I have nothing to offer," he told the House of Commons on May 13, "but blood, toil, tears, and sweat."

But, as a writer in *Notes & Queries* (1944) points out, it is likely that Churchill drew, consciously or unconsciously, from the following passage in John Donne's *An Anatomie of the World* (1611):

> Shee, shee is dead; shee's dead; when thou knowst this,
> Thou knowst how drie a Cinder this world is,
> And learn'st thus much by our Anatomy,

That 'tis in vaine to dew, or mollifie
It with thy teares, or sweat, or blood: nothing
Is worth our travaile, griefe, or perishing,
But those rich joyes, which did possesse her heart,
Of which she's now partner, and a part.

Or, perchance, from these satirical lines from Byron's "The Age of Bronze":

Safe in their barns, these Sabine tillers sent
Their brethren out to battle—Why? For rent!
Year after year they voted cent. by cent.,
Blood, sweat, and tear-wrung millions—why? for rent!
They roared, they dined, they drank, they swore they
  meant
To die for England—why then live?—for rent!

stripped to the buff

Buff, as we use it most frequently today, is a color, a light yellow. But it is also the name given to a soft, undyed and unglazed leather, especially a leather made from a buffalo hide, for it was from this leather that the color got its name. Someone, about three hundred years ago, facetiously referred to his own bare skin as his "buff," perhaps because it was tanned by the sun and had the characteristic fuzzy surface of buffalo leather. The name stuck, but is now rarely used except in the phrase above, which, of course, means divested of one's clothing.

to sleep like a top

To sleep so soundly as to be utterly quiescent. Efforts have been made to derive the "top" in this saying from the French *taupe*, mole, and thus imply that one sleeps as quietly as a mole; but this solution does not hold, for the French idiom is not *dormir comme une taupe*, but *dormir comme un sabot*, in which *sabot* means a top. The saying has been in English literature since the late seventeenth century, and from its first appearance the evidence is that the analogy refers to the state of apparent immobility of a rapidly spinning top.

hue and cry

Nowadays this just means a great to-do over some matter, especially one accompanied by clamor. But originally, and at least until the early part of the nineteenth century, it was the outcry raised by one who had been robbed, or by the constable or other officer of the law, calling upon all honest men to join in the chase and capture of the thief. One who failed to join the chase was liable to punishment. The expression is very old, dating back at least to the time of Edward I, or the late thirteenth century. In Norman-English spelling it was *hu e cri*, and it seems probable that the ancient meaning of "hue," in this saying, was a whistling or the sound of a horn, or a yell or hoot of some recognized nature, which was followed by a cry such as, "Stop thief! Stop thief!"

a wild-goose chase

Back in Shakespeare's time this was a game played on horseback, with two or more players. It began, apparently, with a race to see which player could take the lead; then, willy-nilly, the losers followed him at set intervals wherever he might choose to lead. The name came from the resemblance to wild geese in flight, each following the leader and at an even distance from one another. It is this game that is referred to in the dialog between Mercutio and Romeo, in Act II, scene 4, of *Romeo and Juliet*. Mercutio says, "Nay, if thy wits run the wild-goose chase, I have done; for thou hast more of the wild-goose in one of thy wits than, I am sure, I have in my whole five: was I with you there for the goose?" Romeo answers, "Thou wast never with me for anything when thou wast not there for the goose." And this style of repartee continues for another thirty lines or so.

But that sport went out of fashion within a few years and was remembered only as representing a wilful and erratic course taken by those who indulged in the chase. By the middle of the eighteenth century, even that much of the origin of the name was forgotten, and, in 1755, Dr. Samuel Johnson defined wild-goose chase as, "A pursuit of something as unlikely to be caught as a wild goose." This has come to be the accepted meaning—a vain pursuit of something, which, even if attained, would be worthless.

to have an ax to grind

To flatter a person or to be obsequious when seeking a favor from him. It is from a story entitled, "Who'll turn the grindstone?" first published in the Wilkesbarre *Gleaner* in 1811, often credited to Benjamin Franklin, but actually written by Charles Miner. It purports to relate an incident in the boyhood of the author: One morning a man with an ax over his shoulder greeted the boy most pleasantly and asked if his father had a grindstone. When the boy said, "Yes," the man complimented him upon his good looks and intelligence and asked if he might borrow the use of the stone. The boy, flattered by the attention, was sure that he could. The man then remarked that the boy appeared to be unusually strong for his age. Of course, the  lad fell for all this flattery, and before he knew it he had been inveigled into turning the stone until the very dull ax was as sharp as a razor. Just then the school bell was heard to ring; the man's manner changed abruptly, and without a word of thanks or a coin, he berated the boy for being a sluggard and ordered him to be off instantly so as not to be late for school. The author closed his tale with the comment, "When I see a merchant over-polite to his customers, begging them to taste a little brandy and throwing half his goods on the counter—thinks I, that man has an ax to grind." The story was reprinted later in a collection, *Essays from the Desk of Poor Robert the Scribe*, confused by many persons with *Poor Richard's Almanac* and for that reason associated with Franklin.

hand over fist (or hand)

At first, this was a nautical expression with a very literal meaning —advancing the hands alternately, as in climbing a rope, hoisting a sail, or the like. Then, still nautical, it acquired a figurative sense— advancing continuously, as if by pulling something toward one by a rope. Thus, in overtaking another vessel rapidly, one spoke of coming up with it "hand over hand." In America, early in the nineteenth century, this second meaning acquired a further extension—hauling in rapidly, as if by reeling in a fish; and, Americans being flippant, the second "hand" became "fist," so that now we say of a friend that he is making money "hand over fist" when his fortunes are in the ascendency.

to get (*set,* or *put*) *one's back up*

Cats have been doing this, when angry, as long as there has been a feline family; but, from the written evidence, it has been only some two centuries that human beings have figuratively been arching their backs when aroused into anger.

to keep the wolf from the door

Because the wolf, from remote antiquity, has been noted for its ravenous appetite, seemingly never able to get enough to eat, it has

always stood as a symbol for hunger, for want and necessity, in English as well as in other languages. The figurative intent was so well understood as far back as 1457 that John Hardyng saw no cause to explain his meaning when, in his *Chronicle,* he wrote, "Endowe hym now, with noble sapience By whiche he maye the wolf werre (ward off) frome the gate."

room to swing a cat

Space in which to move around freely. This is generally used in the negative, "no room to swing a cat," meaning cramped quarters. It was a common saying, according to the records, as long ago as the middle of the seventeenth century, and the origin is not certain. The popular notion is that "cat," in the phrase, was originally a contraction of "cat-o-nine-tails," but this could not be so, for this instrument of punishment was not in use until about a hundred years after the phrase was first recorded.

Of course, the original phrase may have been literal—room in which to hold a cat by the tail and swing it around one's head—but I find it difficult to think of a reason for indulging oneself in this form of exercise. I think instead that it originated in the ancient archery sport to which Shakespeare refers in *Much Ado about Nothing*, where Benedick says, "Hang me in a bottle like a cat, and shoot at me," the "bottle" here being a leather sack in which a live cat was placed to make a swinging target when the sack was hung from a tree. Thus, I think, "room to swing a cat" meant space enough to use for such archery practice.

to fish in troubled waters

"Troubled waters" is itself an idiomatic phrase, used since the sixteenth century to mean mental perturbation or disquiet. And at about the same period our ancestors fished in the same kind of water; that is, they took advantage of another's mental perturbation to gain something desirable for themselves. The earliest instance of use thus far located is in Richard Grafton's *Chronicle of England*, "Their perswasions whiche alwayes desyre your unquietnesse, whereby they may the better fishe in the water when it is troubled." The allusion is to the fact that, as fishermen know, fish bite best when the water is rough.

to paint the town red

Nowadays this has no greater significance than to go on a spree, usually in company with others of like mind. As far as the records go, the term is less than a hundred years old, but as is so often the case, usage probably antedates the printed record by several generations. I think it likely that the first town that was painted red was one actually fired by American Indians on the warpath, one outlined by the pigment of red flame. Figurative paint was probably applied, in later years, by young cowboys from outlying ranches who, bent on riotous revelry, rode into the main streets of a town whooping at the top of their lungs and firing their guns into the air as if actually a band of Comanches.

But Professor T. F. Crane, of Cornell, formerly president of the American Folklore Society, offered the opinion some twenty years ago that the peoples of the earth since the dawn of time have used "red" as a symbol of violence; hence that the expression is a natural figure of speech, signifying "to do violence in town."

too big for one's breeches

A youngster, or an adult for that matter, who struts around trying to impress others with his importance, is said to be "too big for his breeches." Just as with the independent hog on his chunk of ice, this expression gives us another instance of an absurdly recent first appearance in print of an obviously old expression. The first

 appearance is credited to H. G. Wells, and as recently as 1905. But the expression was in use in America before 1850, at least in the Ohio farming region in which my mother was raised, and is undoubtedly much earlier, probably going back to the eighteenth or even the seventeenth century. "Too big for one's boots," very probably a euphemism of the vulgar "breeches," was respectable enough to appear in print by 1879. Today we have moved to the other extreme: he of the swelled buttocks of 1850, of the swelled foot of 1880, is now called a swellhead, or is said to have a head too big for his hat.

a horse of another color

Something of a different nature from that under consideration. Just how long it has been that this phrase has had such a meaning is anyone's guess. It was known by Shakespeare, though he used it as "a horse of the same color" when describing the plot hatched up by Sir Andrew Aguecheek and Sir Toby Belch, in *Twelfth Night*, to get Malvolio in Dutch with his mistress, Olivia. Shakespeare didn't explain the meaning, so it must have been well known to his audiences, but there is no earlier record of its use.

The probabilities are that the expression was a natural statement, possibly made by some favorite princess at a tournament or a race. She may have thought that her favored knight or horse was losing, when, seeing otherwise by better view, she exclaimed, "Oh, but that is a horse of another color!" Delighted courtiers would have repeated the saying on all occasions. Or, perhaps, the saying may have been derived from the archeological mystery, the celebrated White Horse of Berkshire. This is a crudely delineated figure, on an enormous scale, of a galloping horse, excavated in the chalk of a hill in western Berkshire. It is 374 feet long, covering about two acres of ground. Legend attributes the figure to a commemoration of the victory of King Ethelred and his brother Alfred (later, Alfred the Great) over the Danes in 871, but the figure is unmistakably of much greater antiquity. It would have become undistinguishable from the surrounding terrain many centuries ago, however, were it not for the custom of the people of the neighborhood to make it "a horse of another color" periodically by cleaning out the grass and debris from the trenches by which the figure is outlined.

to go against the grain

In wood, the fibers are arranged in parallel lines which run lengthwise along the line of growth of the original tree, and this we call the grain of the wood. The wood may be easily split, sawed, or planed along those parallel lines, or, as we say, "with the grain." We use "against the grain" to describe a cut that runs transversely across those lines, whether at right angles or obliquely. It is the long oblique cut that tends to produce slivers; one's fingers or a plane run smoothly in one direction over such a cut, but snags upon splinters if run in the other direction. This latter direction is more explicitly described as "against the grain," and from it we derive our figurative saying, "to go against the grain," by which we mean to be opposite to one's inclination or preference, or, especially, to be repugnant to one's feelings.

to catch a Tartar

To have a bull by the tail; to stir up a hornet's nest, or, in plain English, to take something that one expects to be advantageous and find it to be an unpleasant attachment that one cannot be rid of— like marrying a woman for her· money and finding her to be not only miserly, but also a nagging scold. The saying seems not to be older than about the middle of the seventeenth century; Dryden was the first to record it. But for its source we can do no better than, with tongue in cheek, to repeat the story given by Francis Grose in his *Classical Dictionary of the Vulgar Tongue*, published in 1785. He says, "This saying originated from a story of an Irish soldier in the Imperial service, who, in a battle against the Turks, called out to his comrade that he had caught a Tartar. 'Bring him along, then,' said he. 'He won't come,' answered Paddy. 'Then come along yourself,' replied his comrade. 'Arrah,' cried he, 'but he won't let me.' "

to beat about the bush

So far as I know, batfowling was never an American sport. Perhaps game has always been too plentiful. But we have to go way back to this ancient practice in the fifteenth century for the origin of this expression. Batfowling was nothing more than the hunting of birds at night, the hunter armed with a light with which to  dazzle the sleepy birds, and a bat with which to kill them. (The next day they formed his repast, ba-ked in a pye!) Or, in some instances, the hunter would use a net for trapping the birds, hiring a boy or someone else, armed with a bat, to stir up the birds asleep in a bush. The birds, attracted by the light, would fly toward it and become entangled in the net. When there were more birds in a flock than could roost on a single bush, the batfowlers usually beat the bushes adjacent to the one on which the main flock was asleep, thus literally beating about the bush to reach their main objective. So when today Junior says, "Daddy, are you going to use the car tonight?" we recognize that, like the batfowlers of old, he is "beating about the bush," approaching indirectly the subject he has in mind.

to lick into shape

This we do when we take something formless or not fully in readiness to meet the critical eyes of the world and put it into form or make it ready. The saying comes from the ancient belief that, to quote from the unknown translator (about 1400) of de Guilleville's *The pylgremage of the sowle*, "Beres (bears) ben brought forthe al fowle and transformyd (are born all foul and shapeless) and after that by lyckynge of the fader and moder (by licking of the father and mother) they ben brought in to theyr kyndely shap."

The belief, probably arising from the fact that, at birth, the cubs are hairless and very small, as well as the fact that the mother usually keeps them concealed in her remote den for four or five weeks, is of great antiquity. The saying was used by the Roman writer, Donatus, in discussing the great care taken by Virgil when writing his *Georgics*. He said: "Cum Georgica scriberet, traditur cotidie meditatos mane plurimos versus dictare solitus ac per totum diem retractando ad paucissimos redigere, non absurde carmen se more ursae parere dicens et lambendo demun effingere."

to rule the roost

This is the American expression, and, according to the record, we and our grandsires before us and their sires or grandsires also used it when expressing mastership or authority. The original analogy was, undoubtedly, the rooster, who is cock of the walk in the henyard. It is very likely, however, that the American saying was strongly influenced by the far older British saying which conveys the same meaning, "to rule the roast." And this usage goes back at least to the fifteenth century— "What so euer ye brage or boste, My mayster yet shall reule the roste." The origin of the British expression has caused a great deal of speculation. The usual  assumption is that it alluded to the lord of the manor who presided over the roast of meat at the table; but I find myself in agreement with the minority in the belief that the actual ancient word was that which we pronounce "roost" today. Formerly, along with door, floor, brooch, other words now spelled with a double "*o*" were also pronounced with a long "*o*," and there is excellent reason to suppose that "roost" was one of them. This, together with the fact that modern "roast" was formerly sometimes spelled "roost," makes it fairly convincing to me that the ancient intent was in full accord with the modern American expression, or that the old-time master who exercised full authority, along with the cock of the barnyard, actually "ruled the roost."

a hair of the dog that bit you

Customarily, this applies to a drink taken as a pick-me-up on the morning after a spree, to a drink taken for relief from an excess of drinks. Heywood, in 1546, thus recorded it in his *Dialogue conteynyng prouerbes and epigrammes:* "I pray the leat me and my felow hauę A heare of the dog that bote vs last night—And bitten were we both to the braine aright." The  curious name for the practice comes from a widely accepted medical doctrine that goes back at least to the sixteenth century and was probably the common folk belief many centuries before that. That is, it was generally and seriously believed that if one were bitten by a dog suffering from rabies (by a "mad dog"), one's chance of recovery was greatly improved if a hair from that dog could be secured and bound upon the wound. It may be pertinent to remark that, though this treatment was still recommended up to the middle of the eighteenth century, its efficacy is now doubted; possibly the same could be said of the morning pick-me-up.

gone to Jericho

According to the Bible (II Samuel x), Hanun, to whom David had sent his servants as a mark of respect for Hanun's father, who had just died, was persuaded that they were actually spies; he had them seized, half their beards shaved off, and then sent them back to their master in derision. The servants, ashamed of their disgraced condition, were unwilling to return to Jerusalem and sent word of their plight to David. He sent word back, "Tarry at Jericho until your beards be grown."

But it was a much later king who inspired our present expression. Henry VIII, it is said, had a place of retirement on a small stream called "Jordan," near Chelmsford, which he called "Jericho." Like the servants of David, he may first have gone there to be in seclusion while his beard grew, but his later visits at least, were supposedly in company with a paramour of the moment. At any rate, his courtiers and ministers recognized that, officially, no one knew where the king might be whenever his servants announced that he had "gone to Jericho." It is for that reason that the expression has come to mean any indefinite or nameless place.

to give a wide berth to

The word "berth" came into the language early in the seventeenth century from sources unknown. It was a nautical term employed to mean roomway for a ship in which to operate. The early phrase was "to give a good (or, a clear) berth to," which meant, literally, to avoid, or to keep well away from, and we give it the same meaning today, though rarely with reference to a ship.

to put the screws on

Among the instruments of torture used, especially in Scotland, in the late seventeenth century was the screw or thumbscrew. It was a clamp or vise applied to one or both thumbs of the victim which could be tightened under the slow and inexorable pressure of a screw. The device was used for extorting confession from an accused, or for exacting money from a victim. Another name for the device was the thumbikins, and an earlier machine, probably intended for compressing the fingers, was known as the pilliwinks.

One who has suffered the accident of having his (or, more likely, her) fingers caught in an electrically operated clothes wringer can faintly imagine the continued and excruciating agony of relentlessly applied compression of the thumbs. To one who had once suffered the agony, no more than a threat to "put the screws on" was probably necessary to compel acquiescence. Memory of the torture survives only in the phrase which we use to indicate moral, rather than physical pressure.

like a Trojan

According to legend, the people of Troy, especially those who accompanied Paris in his abduction of Helen, were endowed with prodigious strength, endurance, energy, and capacity. English acceptance of the legend dates back to the Benedictine chronicler of the fourteenth century, Ranulf Higden; but it was not until the nineteenth century that English and American writers began to compare the powers of their fictional heroes—for lying, for working, for drinking, and even for swearing—with these Trojan heroes.

an itching foot

Though it is only within the past fifty years, apparently, that we in America have used this to mean a craving to travel, we have  ancient precedent for such a figurative expression. Away back in the thirteenth century a writer used "an itching ear" to mean a craving to hear gossip, and, later, one with "an itching tongue" was one with an inordinate desire to repeat gossip. Even today one with "an itching palm" craves money. There seems no end to the itching that one may have.

in apple-pie order

That which is said to be "in apple-pie order" has a perfection of orderliness, but no one has been able to figure out the reason for this with certainty. The expression is of British origin, and has been used since early in the nineteenth century at least. Some have tried to figure that it may have been derived from "cap-a-pie," which, in English usage, means "from head to foot," but there is no known instance of such an expression as "cap-a-pie order," and the expression itself seems meaningless. A very recent philologist, Bruce Chapman, asserts confidently: "The phrase comes from the French *nappes pliées*, meaning 'folded linen,' " but he does not cite any instance of the use of this French phrase in English literature, and, unable to find any instance myself, I cannot support his derivation, plausible though it may appear. If only some cookbook of, say, 1800 could be found, possibly we might learn that some unusually finicky cook had prescribed a most precise manner or arrangement in which an apple pie should properly be concocted, so precise as to earn the derision of all proficient cooks who thereupon made "apple-pie order" notorious.

full as a tick

Some suppose that the tick to which this simile alludes is the bed-tick, the old-fashioned flat, rectangular bag of cloth which was stuffed with feathers, straw, or the like to form a bed. It had to be full, of course, or one might find one's poor bones resting on the floor. But the tick that is really meant is the disgusting, bloodsucking insect that attacks the skin of man or other animal, burying its head into the flesh and becoming fat and bloated.

to grease (a person's) palm

When you enrich someone with money in the hope or expectation of having a favor from him in return, you "grease his palm." The present expression has been in vogue since the beginning of the eighteenth century, changed since the early sixteenth century only in the substitution of "palm" for "hand." Our present form, however, is a direct translation of a French phrase of the Middle Ages, "oindre la paume à quelqu'un." Littré, the French philologist, tells of an ancient story about an old woman whose two cows had been seized by the provost and who then received the advice that she would have saved herself from trouble had she first "greased his palm."

to bring down the house

To call forth such wild applause, as at a theater, that the very walls seem to tremble and be about to fall. Possibly this could be done actually, for, we are told, a regiment marching in cadence across a bridge could cause its destruction. I have not heard, however, that applause has ever been so continuous and tumultuous as that. Perhaps the expression was used by those who described the effect of a play by Will Shakespeare upon his audience, but, if so, no one thought to record it. Its first use in print did not come until more than a century after Shakespeare died.

to cut the coat according to the cloth

A tailor, making such a coat, would pay no attention to the pattern in the cloth nor to warp or woof; he would make it out of  whatever material there was at hand, taking advantage of every scrap, regardless of the appearance of the ultimate garment. It is likely that tailors—and mothers—have been thus adapting themselves to circumstances—which is the meaning of the phrase—since Jacob made Joseph a patchwork coat of many colors, for the saying has great age. It had become proverbial in England by the time Heywood compiled his *Dialogue conteynyng Prouerbes and Epigrammes* in 1546, but no one can tell how much earlier it had been in common English speech.

blind tiger

This name for a place where liquor is illegally sold is scarcely more than sixty years old, though the reason for the appellation can now only be surmised. I think it likely that the "blind tiger" began its career in the back room of a faro establishment, for this game was known more than a hundred years ago, in America, as "tiger." As the game itself was often conducted illegally, it would be perfectly in keeping that a second license for selling booze in a "blind tiger" would not be secured.

We have the game of faro to thank also for "to buck the tiger." In less picturesque words this means to play against the bank; hence, to gamble. This, too, was known a century ago. According to Walsh, *Appleton's Journal* traced "tiger" to a figure of a tiger appearing with one of the Chinese gods of chance; the figure, it is said, is used in China as a sign before the entrance to a gambling house.

to hold one's horses

Originally, this had nothing but its literal meaning—to keep one's team of horses from getting excited. In the United States somewhat more than a hundred years ago, however, the expression began to be applied to people, always as a mild adjuration. And because of an assumed rustic source, the suggestion that one control one's temper or patience is generally phrased, placatingly, "Now, just hold your hosses."

to run (something) into the ground

Bartlett, back in 1859, thought that this American phrase probably came from hunting, "to express the earthing of a fox or other game." But because the sense has always been to overdo (a matter), to carry (something) to extremes, Bartlett's explanation fails to satisfy. In my opinion, the phrase was probably of nautical origin. It may have been said of an eager youngster learning to sail, or even of an experienced helmsman who, upon reaching his home port after a long voyage, had so strong a desire to see his family as to overshoot the landing. Thus, in an excess of zeal, one might literally run (a vessel) into the ground.

ghost writer

Ghosts, as everyone knows, are invisible, unseen. So it is with the ghost writer; he is the unseen anonymous person who actually writes for hire or love the articles or the speeches that a prominent person gets the credit for having written. Until a decade or so ago such persons, from about 1850, were just called ghosts—somebody thought it a bit more dignified to add "writer."
In fact, ghostwriting is an honorable profession these days. Recent presidents, engrossed upon important affairs of state, have had no time to prepare public speeches that are, say, primarily political in nature. Someone who is familiar with the views of the important person is called upon to write the speech that will be used, but the public is led to believe that the important personage has himself written the speech. Ghost-

writing has become such a profession these days that ghosts may be found who, for a price, will write a speech, an essay, or an article upon any given subject. Even an occasional book, ascribed to some "big shot," is actually the work of a ghost.

manna from heaven

A windfall; something providential. That is the current figurative use of the expression; but, as any biblical student knows, the real manna from heaven was that spoken of in the sixteenth chapter of Exodus, "a small round thing, as small as the hoar frost on the ground," which provided the needed food for the children of Israel on their journey out of Egypt.

in the dog house

Aside from the literal sense, this modern expression is used to mean that a person is undergoing punishment of some sort. It is usually used to denote the treatment, mental or physical, meted out to a man by his spouse for some misdemeanor. Probably the original allusion was to a "gay dog," a man who, in his wife's opinion, had been somewhat too gay and jovial, or perhaps had been roving too far from his own fireside. And, just as the punishment for a roving dog is to be confined to his kennel, so the two-legged gay dog deserved similar treatment.

a month of Sundays

This has become just a glib expression for a long time. But when coined, a hundred years ago—first as "a week of Sundays," then, in amplification, as "a month of Sundays"—it meant an interminable length of time, especially to a young person—and possibly, if the truth were known, to many an older person. In those days a well brought-up person was obliged to observe Sunday with the utmost decorum; not only no games, but no levity was permitted. To a child or young person of any spirit, the day seemed never ending. The utmost of dreariness, a veritable eternity to such a person would be seven or thirty Sundays in succession.

to play fast and loose

When something has been promised and the promise is accepted in good faith, but never fulfilled, he who made the promise has "played fast and loose" with the person to whom it was made; that is, he was not trustworthy. The expression was the name of a game known and played as far back as the first half of the sixteenth century. It was a cheating game played at village fairs by sharpers, usually gipsies. A belt or strap was doubled and coiled in such a manner that, when laid edgewise, it appeared to have a loop in its center. That was the trick; for the loop seemed to be so definitely a loop that it was not difficult to persuade a rustic that he could easily fasten the belt to the table by running a skewer through the loop. After bets were placed the sharper skilfully unrolled the belt, which had had no loop in it at all. The game must have been quite popular, for it was mentioned by many writers of the period. Shakespeare spoke of it in *King John*, in *Love's Labor's Lost*, and in *Antony and Cleopatra*. In more recent years the same trick has been known as "Prick the Loop," or "Prick the Garter."

hell for leather

In America we'd say, "in a hell of a hurry," with the same meaning; but this is a British expression, apparently originating in the British army in India. Possibly Kipling coined it, for he was the first to record it, though he may have been actually quoting army speech. His first usage is in *The Story of the Gadsbys*, in that portion of the story ("The Valley of the Shadow") where Mrs. Gadsby is just emerging from "the Valley." His second use of the expression is in Mulvaney's episode with "My Lord the  Elephant," in *Many Inventions*. Though the term must originally have referred to the terrific beating inflicted upon leather saddles by heavy troopers at full speed, even by Kipling's time it had acquired a figurative sense indicating great speed, on foot, by vehicle, or by horse.

to hold a candle to (someone)

This is usually in the negative—so-and-so can't, or isn't fit to, or isn't able to hold a candle to such and such—and we mean that the party of the first part fares poorly by comparison with the party of the second part. The development of the present-day simile came somewhat gradually from an ordinary custom of the sixteenth century and later. Because of poorly lighted streets it was customary for a servitor with a lighted candle to accompany his master when on foot. It was a menial service, one that required no training nor skill, nothing more than familiarity with the way. One who did not know the road was, literally, not fit to or not worthy to hold a candle to a superior. But by the eighteenth century, the sense of worthiness or of comparative ability had become the intent of the phrase, as illustrated by John Byrom's "Epigram on the Feuds between Handel and Bononcini," printed in a 1725 issue of the *London Journal*:

> *Some say, that Seignior Bononchini*
> *Compar'd to Handel's a mere Ninny;*
> *Others aver, to him, that Handel*
> *Is scarcely fit to hold a candle.*
> *Strange! that such high Disputes shou'd be*
> *'Twixt Tweedledum and Tweedledee.*

The positive expression, "to hold a candle to (someone)," was, literally, to act as an assistant to one by holding a light for him. In our present electric-lighted age we do not appreciate the inadequacy of candles for illumination until some emergency obliges us to return to them. On such occasion, if we try to play cards we find that candles not only interfere with our arms, but that the light falls in the eyes of the players rather than on the cards. Our ancestors, who had no better light than candles, had the same difficulty. Hence, when playing cards or dicing, they employed a servitor to hold the light where needed, paying him for both his services and the light. So when the game was going poorly or indifferently, one might find that one's winnings were too light to defray these expenses. This literal fact gave birth to the proverb, "the game is not worth the candle," which we use conveniently to mean that the returns from a given enterprise are not worth the effort expended upon it.

to cut didos

This is something that a Britisher doesn't do. He cuts a caper or otherwise cavorts around. There is nothing to show that George Washington cut any didos, though it is likely that others were doing so during the latter part of his life, for probably the expression was coined about that time. It was widely enough known to be used in *A Narrative of the Life & Travels of John Robert Shaw, the Well-Digger*, an autobiography published in 1807. Whoever coined the dido left us no certain clue of its origin; he may have alluded in some manner to the trick performed by the mythological queen, Dido, who founded Carthage. When she landed in Africa, according to the story, she bought from the trusting natives only the land that could be enclosed with a bull's hide. Having agreed upon the price, the crafty queen then proceeded to cut the bull's hide into a continuous cord slightly thicker than a hair, and thus encircled enough land upon which to build the walled city of Carthage. Some dido!

to pull the wool over one's eyes

A very roundabout way of saying to hoodwink, to delude. The expression is said to have originated in the United States, probably because the earliest use of the expression in print that has yet been found is American. But this was in a newspaper, so it must have been widely known at that time, 1839, because the meaning was not explained. The actual source was likely to have been much earlier, and perhaps in England. Quite probably, "wool" was jocularly used for hair, and perhaps for the hair that composed a wig. Hence, the expression may have originated in a practice, either sportive or malicious, of pulling the wig of some nabob over his eyes to blind him temporarily, perhaps for the purpose of snatching his purse, or perhaps just teasingly.

to be caught with one's pants down

When such a respectable family publication as *The Saturday Evening Post* gives its sanction to this homely American expression, notice of its origin may properly be taken. Despite the fact that the appearance of the phrase in the *Post* is its first in print (1946), so far as is known, in all likelihood its popular usage goes back a hundred years. Maybe longer. Maybe it was anciently "to be caught with one's breeches down"; but the expression was never considered to be decorous enough to appear in print, so we cannot be certain of its age.

The figurative meaning is, of course, to be taken completely by surprise; to be wholly unprepared. But the literal meaning, I think, takes us back to the days when white frontiersmen were exposed to peril if their muskets were not actually at hand. Even at the risk of death, the wants of nature must be met, and in such circumstances a lurking Indian would indeed catch one in a state of embarrassing unpreparedness.

cock of the walk

This is he who "rules the roost," who permits no doubt of his supremacy. The figurative use is so common, especially as applied to a young dandy strutting along the sidewalk, that we are not likely to wonder why a rooster would be upon a promenade nor how long its cockiness would last if it were. But, especially in England, "walk" has a particular application. It means a place set aside for the feeding and exercise of domestic animals; or, in this instance, a chicken yard. The literal cock of the walk, therefore, is the rooster in a given chicken yard. The figurative expression seems to have been in use little more than a century.

to keep one's fingers crossed

This we do, either actually or mentally, when wishing the success of something or hoping that nothing unpleasant will happen or anything will interfere with one's plans. The expression appears to be wholly American and, probably, of Negro origin. Probably it arose from the superstition that making the sign of the cross would avert evil; hence, that it would bring good luck.

In all likelihood the firm belief among American children that a lie doesn't count as a lie if one's fingers are crossed while it is being spoken, comes from the same superstition. That is, as every child knows, some dire punishment is likely to be meted out if one tells a lie; but, since evil may be averted if a cross be made of one's fingers, therefore, by specious reasoning, if one is not punished for the telling, no lie has been told.

brass hat

The modern extension of this slang appellation means any person in authority, especially one who has an overbearing manner. Originally it was British army slang; one of the earliest instances of its literary use was by Kipling, in *Many Inventions*, in 1893, in the story, "In the Rukh." Soldiers used it to designate a general, because the quantity of gold braid about that officer's dress cap made it shimmer in the sun as if the entire cap were of shiny brass. Kipling puts it into the speech of the head ranger of all India, a gigantic German in the British service, and the manner of use indicates that the appellation was already in wide use. The German, Muller, explaining his theory that best efficiency  among subordinates is obtained by visiting them unexpectedly, says: "If I only talk to my boys like a Dutch uncle, dey say, 'It was only dot damned old Muller,' and dey do better next dime. But if my fathead clerk he write and say dot Muller der Inspecdor-General fail to onderstand and is much annoyed, first dot does no goot because I am not dere, and, second, der fool dot comes after me he may say to my best boys: 'Look here, you haf been wigged by my bredecessor.' I tell you der big brass-hat pizness does not make der trees grow."

to put a spoke in one's wheel

Whenever you are not in accord with another person's plans or projects, you "put a spoke in his wheel" by taking some action that will interfere with or impede his progress. The expression goes back to the sixteenth century and alluded to the use, by carters, of an extra spoke or bar which could be thrust between the spokes of a wheel so that that wheel would drag and serve as a brake in descending a hill.

to keep under one's hat

One would suppose that this warning would be as old as the first hat, but its actual history appears to have been no earlier than the closing years of the nineteenth century. What is kept under the hat, of course, is retained within the head; that is, it remains a secret.

up the spout

When we say that something is or has gone "up the spout," we mean, usually, that plans have gone awry, that affairs are hopeless. This is literal as well as figurative, for "spout" is slang for a pawnbroker's shop, to which we turn when things are desperate and we need cash. Mr. Pickwick, as readers of Dickens' works will know, discovered that meaning when he visited Fleet Prison to see his friend, Mr. Alfred Jingle, who, imprisoned for debt, had pawned his coat, boots, and other raiment for food; he had sent them, Jingle said, to "Spout—dear relation—uncle Tom."

The real spout was, in former days, the hoist or elevator within a pawnbroker's shop by which articles pawned were carried to an upper floor for storage. Such articles literally went "up the spout." The literal meaning is old enough to have been recorded in *A new and comprehensive vocabulary of the flash language* by James H. Vaux in 1812.

to rob Peter to pay Paul

Speculation has been rife for centuries over the origin of this common saying; every avenue has apparently been explored, but the original allusion is still a mystery. In English it dates back at least to the fourteenth century; the French have a similar saying at least as old, and there is, in Latin, a twelfth-century phrase, "Tanquam si quis crucifigeret Paulum ut redimeret Petrum, (As it were that one would crucify Paul in order to redeem Peter)." The verbs have varied from time to time, depending upon the desired application. Thus we find that one has borrowed from or unclothed Peter to pay or to clothe Paul, but "rob" is the oldest English usage, so recorded in Wyclif's *Select English Works*, written about 1380. The thought has always been, to take something (usually money) that is needed for one purpose and use it for another.

to drag a red herring over the track (or trail)

Red herring is nothing more than herring that has been cured by smoke, a process that changes the color of the flesh to a reddish hue. The herring is intended to be eaten after such curing, but dog trainers learned long ago that red herring had a peculiarly persistent odor and was very useful, if trailed over the ground, for training a dog to follow a scent. The author of *The Gentlemen's Recreation*, in 1686, advised that if a dog could not be trained by dragging a dead cat or dead fox, a red herring, having a more powerful odor,  could be employed, and it could not fail to serve the desired purpose. But that which leaves so strong a scent can be used for bad purposes as well as good. A dog that gets a good whiff of red herring will lose any other scent that it has been following. Criminals who have been chased by bloodhounds have used that knowledge to advantage. So when our small son, trying to divert our attention from the pink stickiness on his cheek, shows us the daub of jam on the cat's back, we accuse him of dragging a red herring over the track, figuratively, by trying to turn our suspicions aside.

to get (or give one) the sack

Cotgrave, in his *Dictionaire of the French and English Tongues*, published in 1611, shows us that we are still using, by translation, an expression known to the French more than three centuries ago. The same saying in Dutch is used in the Netherlands and can be traced there back to the Middle Dutch. It meant, in all cases, to be dismissed (or to dismiss one) from employment.

Because the expression goes back to the Middle Ages, the theory has been advanced that the "sack" was one in which an itinerant worker carried his tools and, if his work were unsatisfactory, he would receive notification thereof by the return of his sack by his employer. That explanation would carry the implication that it was the custom for all workmen to leave their tools lying around unprotected, which is highly improbable. It would also imply that the craft guilds had sent forth an unprepared master workman.

Evidence is lacking, but I think it probable that the "sack" of the Middle Ages was always figurative, that it alluded to the ancient Roman punishment of putting a condemned person into a sack and drowning him in the Tiber. That form of punishment was common throughout Europe in the Middle Ages and persisted in Turkey until the nineteenth century. The figurative usage may have begun as a threat of fatal punishment, just as today we "fire" an employee when he is discharged, likening him to the bullet sent away, or fired, or discharged from a gun.

a gone coon

Legend has it that this expression, which is applied to a person or thing in a hopeless situation, originated in the Revolutionary War. An American spy, it is said, seeking information on the number of British forces that were to be attacked, dressed himself in raccoon furs and, by night, stealthily climbed a tree overlooking the British camp. He hoped that the protective coloration of the fur would shield him from discovery. To his dismay, however, he had scarcely taken his position when a British soldier, on a nocturnal raccoon hunt, approached the tree and spotted what he supposed to be an unusually large specimen of this tasty animal. The Briton took careful aim and was just about to fire, when the American called out, "Don't shoot! I'll come down. I know I'm a gone coon." It so terrified the Briton to hear a raccoon talk, the legend goes, that he dropped his gun and ran away in panic.

But Captain Frederick Marryat, British author, who wrote a notably fair *Diary in America*, in 1839, had not heard this alleged earlier version. When he asked what the origin of the expression was, he was told that it was attributed to a certain Captain Martin Scott of Vermont, an army officer with a prodigious reputation as a sharpshooter. According to the story that was told:

His fame was so considerable that even the animals were aware of it. He went out one morning with his rifle, and spying a raccoon upon the upper branches of a high tree, brought his gun up to his shoulder; when the raccoon perceiving it, raised his paw for a parley. "I beg your pardon, mister," said the raccoon, very politely; "but may I ask if your name is Scott?"—"Yes," replied the captain— "Martin Scott?" continued the raccoon—"Yes," replied the captain —"Captain Martin Scott?" still continued the animal—"Yes," replied the captain, "Captain Martin Scott"—"Oh! then," says the animal, "I may just as well come down, for I'm a gone coon."

to be neither fish nor flesh

No evidence has been found, either in proof or denial, yet the fact that the earliest record of this phrase coincided almost exactly with the break between Henry VIII and the Pope, a break that could not have occurred unless preceded by a long period of disaffection, makes me suspect that the original significance of the expression was theological. One who abstained from neither fish nor flesh when days of fasting were prescribed were neither Roman Catholics nor Dissenters, neither one thing nor the other—just plain irreligious. Merely to intensify a lack of distinction indicated by the phrase, someone appended, "nor good red herring." This is not a recent appendage, for it was recorded as long ago as 1546 by John Heywood, in his *Dialogue conteynyng Prouerbes and Epigrammes*. Probably because herring is not as popular in the United States as in England, we have substituted "fowl" for "red herring" and, unaware of early significance, when anything cannot be definitely classified or its nature fixed, we say that it is "neither fish, flesh, nor fowl."

to let the old cat die

Both in England and America when one permits a swing to come to rest one "lets the old cat die," yet no one knows positively why this saying is used. It seems to be so old that the original allusion is lost. In my opinion, however, it comes from the same source as the other common saying, "room to swing a cat." We may find it hard to realize now, but the time was not very remote when no one was at all concerned over the sufferings of dumb animals. Thus, as Shakespeare reports in *Much Ado about Nothing*, there was an ancient archery sport in which a cat was put into a sack (a leather bottle, according to Shakespeare) which, in turn, was suspended from a tree; the efforts of the cat to escape provided a swinging target. Probably it was no part of the sport to kill the cat, but it is more than likely that the poor beast was at least injured before the marksmen wearied of the sport. So, I think, rather than to open the bag and run the risk of getting severely scratched by the injured animal, both bag and cat were left swinging from the tree until "the old cat died."

straight from the horse's mouth

When we hear someone say he had such and such a piece of information "straight from the horse's mouth," we know that he means that he received it from the highest authority, from the one person whose testimony is beyond question. The expression comes from horse-racing and has to do with the age of the racers. Scientists

tell us that the most certain evidence of the age of a horse is by examination of its teeth, especially those of the lower jaw. The first of its permanent teeth, those in the center of the jaw, do not begin to appear until the animal is two and a half years old. A year later the second pair, those alongside the first, begin to come through, and when the animal is between its fourth and fifth year, the third pair appears. Thus, no matter what an owner may say of the horse's age, by an examination of its lower jaw an experienced person can get his information at first hand, straight from the horse's mouth.

to put one through a course of sprouts

To give one a thorough and disciplined course of training, or, by extension, to give one a grueling examination. What the source may have been cannot now be determined, though the Americanism is not much more than a hundred years old. The "sprouts" could have been children, and the "course of sprouts" could have indicated a severe course of instruction.

caviar to the general

Something that is an acquired taste; something too racy or too unfamiliar to be acceptable to the general public. The expression is from Shakespeare's *Hamlet*, Act II, scene 2, in which Hamlet, speaking of a play, says, ". . . it was never acted . . . the Play I remember pleased not the Million, 'twas Cauiarie to the Generall."

between cup and lip

Four centuries ago the saying was "between cup and mouth," at least it is so recorded in *Prouerbes or Adagies*, by Richard Taverner, published in 1539: "Manye thynges fall betweene ye cuppe and the mouth." The saying itself, however, is much older than that, for Taverner was merely translating into English the Latin collection of adages, *Chiliades adagiorum*, published by Erasmus in 1508. In one form or another, it is found in many languages.

Usually, in English, the saying occurs in the form of a proverb, "There's many a slip between cup and lip," signifying that there is nothing certain in life, that though one may have a cup at his mouth ready to swallow its contents, something may even then prevent the drinking. Erasmus wrote it, "Multa cadunt inter calicem supremaque labra," and is believed to have taken it from Greek. The origin is said to have come from the following legendary incident: Ancæus, a son of Neptune, was especially skilful in the cultivation of his vineyard, and drove his slaves exceedingly hard at this work. One year, a slave, worn out by toil, prophesied that the master would never taste the wine from that harvest; but when the fruit was gathered and the first wine was being pressed from it, Ancæus sent for the slave to show how poor a prophet he was. "There's many a slip between cup and lip," replied the slave as Ancæus raised the goblet to his mouth, and just at that moment another slave rushed up, crying that a wild boar was destroying the vineyard. Ancæus dropped the cup, ran to the fields to drive off the marauder, but the ferocious beast turned upon his pursuer and gored him to death before anyone could come to his aid.

the fat is in the fire

Back in the early sixteenth century when this saying first came into use the meaning of it was that the project, whatever it might have been, had become wholly ruined. The thought was, I suppose, that meat being broiled upon a spit is ruined by the resulting flame if a chunk of the fat drops into the fire. In this original sense the proverb is found in John Heywood's *A Dialogue conteynyng Prouerbes and Epigrammes*, published in 1562. But in the course of the next hundred years the meaning became altered to the present sense, and now we use the phrase to mean that an action of some sort has occurred which will lead to further action or from which great excitement, as of anger or indignation, will result.

Adam's off ox

The form commonly used is "not to know one from Adam's off ox," meaning to have not the slighest information about the person indicated. The saying in any form, however, is another of the numerous ones commonly heard but of which no printed record has been found. But in 1848 the author of a book on *Nantucketisms* recorded a saying then in use on that island, "Poor as God's off ox," which, he said, meant very poor. It is possible that on the mainland "Adam" was used as a euphemistic substitute.

The off ox, in a yoke of oxen, is the one on the right of the team. Because it is the farthest from the driver it cannot be so well seen and may therefore get the worst of the footing. It is for that reason that "off ox" has been used figuratively to designate a clumsy or awkward person.

faster than greased lightning

Denoting the acme of speed, than which nothing could be faster. This appears to be one of the instances of American hyperbole about which British visitors to our shores, a century ago, were always complaining—or secretly envying. Our ancestors, in the days of Washington, Adams, and Jefferson, were not content to indicate great speed in such a trite manner as "faster than lightning"; instead, knowing that a cart with greased wheels will go faster than if the wheels were dry, they merely greased the lightning.

the jumping-off place

Originally, this imaginary place was the edge of the earth, the ultima Thule. From there, one could proceed no farther, other than to leap straight into hell. At least, such appears to have been the thought of our American pioneering forebears in the late eighteenth or early nineteenth century when this description was first applied. Perhaps it was an adaptation from some Indian belief, but, of course, by the early nineteenth century it was applied figuratively to any place, as a God-forsaken town, a desolate waste, any hopeless out-of-the-way spot, which one might deem to be literally next door to hell.

a bad egg; a good egg

A bag egg figuratively is like a bad egg literally—a person, or an egg, that externally appears to be wholesome and sound but, upon closer acquaintance, is found to be thoroughly rotten. By some strange chance this slang usage did not develop until about the middle of the past century, though even Shakespeare called a young person an "egg," as when, in *Macbeth*, the murderers, seeking Macduff, encounter and slay his young son, with the words, "What you egg! Young fry of treachery!"

A good egg, the converse of a bad egg, did not come into popular use until the early part of the present century, and it seems to have first been British university slang, probably first used at Oxford.

to heap coals of fire on one's head

To return good for evil, and thus make the recipient uncomfortable. The passage most often quoted is from the Old Testament,

Proverbs xxv, 21, 22: "If thine enemy be hungry, give him bread to eat; and if he be thirsty, give him water to drink: For thou shalt heap coals of fire upon his head, and the Lord shall reward thee." It is possible that the ancient Hebrew writer had some old metaphor in mind, but the usual explanation of the biblical passage is that the coals of fire upon one's head might melt him into kindliness. It reminds us that our word "remorse," which has a somewhat similar meaning, comes from the Latin *re* plus *morsus*, which has the literal meaning, a biting or gnawing again.

tit for tat

A blow for a blow; an ill deed for an ill deed. This phrase, which expresses a moderate retaliation, goes back only about four centuries in its present form, but before that it was "a tip for a tap," which goes back certainly a hundred years earlier and probably much more than that. A "tip," in Middle English, was a light blow; a "tap," then as now, was also a light blow. So the expression is far weaker than the old Hebrew adage, "an eye for an eye, and a tooth for a tooth." We use it chiefly in reference to speech: an insult for an insult; an unkind remark in return for an unkind remark. Probably the original expression was influenced by the French phrase, *tant pour tant*, literally, so much for so much.

chip of the old block

One who has the characteristics of a parent, usually a son with those of his father. The expression goes back to the early seventeenth  century and, if some of the early sermons of Bishop Robert Sanderson quote it correctly, the original form showed less disrespect to dad. It ran, "chip of the *same* block." The allusion is not difficult to follow: if one takes a block of stone and knocks a chip from it, the chip will carry all the characteristics of the larger portion.

eager beaver

Though its reputation has been questioned in recent years, the beaver has been long noted for persistent industry. This reputation gave us the simile, "to work like a beaver," some two hundred years ago. And, of course, industrious persons have long been likened to the beaver—"So-and-so is a veritable beaver." We English-speaking peoples are gluttons for rimes—as, witness, such compounds as pell-mell, hodge-podge, helter-skelter—so, within the past few years, some bright spirit did the best he could and began referring to some individual who was particularly, and somewhat offensively, avid in his industry as an "eager beaver."

neither hide nor hair

This sounds like such a typically western American expression that it is surprising to find that, though American, it is merely the reverse of one so old that it might have been known to Chaucer. The ancient saying was "in hide and hair," and the meaning was "wholly, entirely." The American phrase means "nothing whatsoever." Our first record of it occurs in one of the early works of Josiah G. Holland, *The Bay Path*, published in 1857: "I havn't seen hide nor hair of the piece ever since." Holland, it may be recalled, wrote under the pen name of Timothy Titcomb and, in 1870, founded *Scribner's Magazine*.

the Brain Trust

Despite the contention that this term was used as a title to a newspaper article in 1903, the name attained no popularity until 1933. In the previous summer, after his nomination for the presidency by the Democratic party, Franklin Delano Roosevelt surrounded himself with a group of advisers to aid in mapping out his election campaign. James M. Kieran of The New York *Times*, assigned to "cover" Mr. Roosevelt at the time, groped for a descriptive name for this group. He tried, it is said, "brains department" but found it too unwieldy, and then hit upon "brains trust." Other reporters ignored his coinage for a time, but after Roosevelt's election and inauguration, when the college professors who had assisted in the campaign were found to have become also a kitchen cabinet of advisers in the administration, Roosevelt himself began to speak of the group as his "brain trust," using the singular form that has since outmoded the original designation. The term is no longer limited in application to a presidential group of advisers, but is applied, sometimes ironically, to any group that establishes the policies of an organization, whether intelligently or not.

to take a message to Garcia

The incident, in time of war, was not unusual; it was not particularly hazardous; but as dramatized by Elbert Hubbard in the March, 1900, issue of his famous magazine, *The Philistine*, it fired the imagination as keenly as if it had been an adventure of a knight of King Arthur's court. The United States, in defense of Cuba, had declared war against Spain. In April, 1898, the American chief of staff wished certain information from the leader of the Cuban forces, General Calixto Garcia, but was unable to establish any communication with him through the Spanish blockade. Accordingly, a young lieutenant, Andrew Rowan, was dispatched from Washington to make his way into Cuba and to find General Garcia, though no one in Washington knew just where the insurgent general might be. Rowan landed secretly on the coast of Cuba in a small boat, learned through local patriots where to look for Garcia, made his way to the general, got the information that he sought, and, with the same privacy, retraced his route to the coast and back to Washington.

The resourcefulness of the young lieutenant was, of course, praiseworthy in the extreme. It was that aspect of the incident which called forth the best of Hubbard's skill. He made it into an impressive sermon to young people, a lesson in success. "To take a message to Garcia" became a byword; it meant, "Show that you are resourceful and inventive, that you can accept responsibilities and can carry them through to success."

sold down the river

Though this is now used with wryful humor, as of a baseball player whose contract is sold to a team of lower rating or of an employee who is transferred to a more humble position than he formerly held, there was a time when it was literal and tragic—when it was used in connection with the domestic slave trade of the southern states. The importation of slaves into the United States was illegal after 1808 (though undoubtedly many thousands were smuggled into the country during the following years) and it then became profitable to build up a domestic trade. Hence, because cotton and sugar plantations of the South and Southwest were expanding by leaps and bounds, slaves from the worn-out tobacco belt of the upper South were readily purchased from their masters by dealers and were then transported down the Mississippi River to the markets at Natchez or New Orleans. Regrettably, many dealers regarded slaves to be as insensitive as cattle, so "sold down the river" meant the loss of all ties, the breaking up of families, and, usually, transportation into the most exhausting of labor under notoriously severe and brutal masters.

cut out of whole cloth

Wholly false; without foundation of truth. Back in the fifteenth century, "whole cloth" was used synonymously with "broad cloth," that is, cloth that ran the full width of the loom. The term dropped into disuse along in the eighteenth century, except in the figurative sense. In early use, the phrase retained much of the literal meaning; a thing was fabricated out of the full amount or extent of that which composed it. Thus we find, in the sixteenth century, "I shalbe contente . . to lende you the choyce of as many gentle wordes and loovelye termes as we . . . use to deliver ower thankes in. Choose whether you will have them given or yeeldid . . . kutt owte of the whole cloathe, or otherwise powrid owte." But by the nineteenth century it would appear that tailors or others who made garments were pulling the wool over the eyes of their customers, for, especially in the United States, the expression came to have just the opposite meaning. Instead of using whole material, as they advertised, they were really using patched or pieced goods, or, it might be, cloth which had been falsely stretched to appear to be of full width.

to get (or give one) the mitten

When a lady fair—an American one—rejects her suitor, she gives him the mitten; he gets it. This has been in American usage for at least a hundred years. *The Knickerbocker*, a  New York periodical, back in July of 1847 wondered how the expression had originated, but it seems clear that the intent of the phrase was that the suitor, requesting the hand of his lady, received instead only it empty, fingerless and insensate covering. The saying apparently has no relationship at all to the medieval custom popularized by Sir Walter Scott. Then, when a knight exhibited his courage and skill in combat upon the jousting field, he might wear or display the glove of the lady of his choice. The meaning then, however, was the reverse of our present phrase.

to get down to brass tacks

Like many other of our common sayings, this appears to have alluded originally to some specific operation, something that would call for the removal of successive layers until the brass tacks which held the structure together were exposed to view. For, as we in America use the expression, it means to get down to the fundamentals, to get to the bottom of a thing, to get to the business at hand. But the original allusion is lost; literary uses have reference only to the figurative sense, and are too recent to afford any clue to the purpose of the first brass tacks. Because tacks, other than ornamental, are made of copper rather than brass, I surmise that "brass" was a figurative use. I think, therefore, that the phrase was originally nautical, that the reference was to the cleaning of the hull of a ship, to scraping the barnacles off so thoroughly as to expose the bolts which held its bottom together. Those bolts were, of course, of copper, but "brass tacks" would be a typical American substitution for "copper bolts." The recently advanced supposition that the saying originated from the brass upholstery tacks placed upon counters in drapers' shops for use in measuring lengths of cloth, seems fanciful to me, for that practice is not old and tacks of that description are of comparatively modern manufacture.

lame duck

In the United States we know a "lame duck" as a congressman who, having run for re-election in November and having been defeated at the polls, still has several months of his term to serve before he bows out more or less gracefully to his successful rival.* But why "lame" and why "duck"? We must go to London for the answer, to a street known as Exchange Alley which, prior to 1773, was the place where London stockbrokers conducted their business. It was the old-time Wall Street of London, and just as we now refer to "the Street," meaning Wall Street, so "the Alley" then meant Exchange Alley. This  alley was the scene of the wildest stock speculation of all time, the noted South Sea Bubble of 1720—stock of the South Sea Company which, in that year, opened at 128½ a share in January, rose to 330 in March, to 550 in May, to 890 in June, and finally touched 1000 a share in July when the directors of the company sold out and the bubble exploded.

Exchange Alley was the place where stockbrokers were first divided into two classes, bears and bulls. And it was also the place which saw, all too frequently, a third class—those who were cleaned out; those who could not meet their financial obligations. These latter came to be known as "lame ducks." Why? Because, to the amused spectator, they "waddled out of the Alley!"

the ghost walks

Salaries are to be paid! The expression is now heard in any line of business: "Friday's the day the ghost walks." "The ghost walks on the fifteenth of each month." The "ghost" is the paymaster, nowadays, or the cashier or whoever may be the distributor of salary or wage. But the expression arose in the theater some ninety years ago, in a profession in which salaries were uncertain and at a time when the whims of the manager might lead to slow pay. The most probable origin of the expression credits it to the actor who, in *Hamlet*,

---

* Although since the passage of the Lame Duck Amendment, the twentieth, in March 1932, lame ducks no longer exist.

had the part of the ghost of Hamlet's father. According to the story, when Hamlet spoke the lines, "I will watch tonight; Perchance t'will walk again," the actor playing the ghost, off stage, shouted back, "I'll be damned if he will unless our salaries are paid."

to knock into a cocked hat

The cocked hat, especially that of the eighteenth and early nineteenth centuries, was permanently out of shape, with the brim turned up along three sides, giving the hat the outline of a triangle. The style was generally affected by officers of both the American and British armies during the Revolutionary War. Undoubtedly the hat was ridiculed by the soldiery, because, in its distorted shape, so much of the hatbrim was wholly useless. Hence, in camp lingo, to knock a fellow soldier into a cocked hat meant that he would be knocked out of shape and rendered useless, and that is still the meaning that we attach to the expression and the meaning in which it first appeared in print, in 1833, when, in depicting American life in his period, it was used by James Kirke Paulding in *Banks of the Ohio*.

Some have credited the expression to a bowling game played in the United States about the middle of the nineteenth century. In this game, only the three corner pins were set up, and the player was allowed three balls to a frame. The name given to the game was "cocked hat," probably in allusion to the triangular arrangement of the pins. But the oldest record of the game is in 1858, so it is unlikely that our phrase was in any way the outcome of this short-lived game.

a man of my kidney

This saying is not now in frequent use; we are much more likely to say, "a man after my own heart," which carries the same meaning. But we find it used by Shakespeare and other writers of bygone years. The explanation takes us back to the philosophy of the Middle Ages, to the time when the temperament of men was supposed to be governed by their "humours." A person who was sullen or gloomy was supposed to have too much black bile, which gives us, from the Greek, the word "melancholy"; one who was irascible was supposed to be bilious, giving us "choler"; one of ruddy complexion was supposed to be cheerful, hopeful, and amorous, hence, full of blood, giving us "sanguine"; one of dull and sluggish nature, or cool and self-possessed, was supposed to have an excess of phlegm, giving us "phlegmatic." In the same philosophy, the kidney was supposed to be the seat of the affections; thus, in the original sense, "a man of my kidney" meant a person whose temperament and disposition were the same as those of the speaker.

to reckon without one's host

To neglect important facts in reaching a conclusion. This seems to have been a failing known also to our remote ancestors; at least, so long ago that the phrase had become proverbial when, in 1489, William Caxton printed (on his new wooden printing press) his own translation of the French *Blanchardyn and Eglantine*. In that early example of English printing may be found the passage, "It ys sayd in comyn that 'who soeuer rekeneth wythoute his hoste, he rekeneth twys for ones.' " But, as shown in this quotation and in others of the next hundred years—"Thei reckened before their host, and so paied more then their shotte came to"; and "He that countis without his oist, Oft tymes he countis twyse"—the tendency of our ancestors, unlike that of the present era, was to include more factors into the reckoning than should have been considered, even "twyse" as many.

to buy a pig in poke

Other languages have similar expressions, all dealing with the folly of buying something that one has not seen. In England, from time immemorial, it has been a pig, a young or suckling pig in a bag, for in ancient days the term "pig" was used only of very young swine, three or four months old, and still small enough to be carried to market slung over the shoulder in a stout "poke," the old-fashioned name for a bag smaller than a sack. The peasantry was apparently not above taking a runt to market and trying to sell it without opening the bag, because, as was undoubtedly the excuse, everyone knew how hard it would be to catch the piglet if it got loose. But the peasantry was also not above other tricks. Some investigators into bygone practices allege that, instead of a runt, it was a cat that was offered to the unwary customer. This view is supported by the French saying, "acheter chat en poche (to buy a cat in a sack)," a saying used, in translation, by John Wyclif in the fourteenth century. A canny purchaser, doubting the integrity of the dealer, however, might refuse to buy without an examination of the contents, thus giving rise to the related saying, "to let the cat out of the bag."

There was also an ancient saying, "When the pig is offered, hold open the poke." It's meaning was to be quick to seize an opportunity when it is offered. The allusion was again to the elusiveness of a pig; if not seized and put into the purchaser's bag, or if the bag were not fully open to receive it, the buyer's chance of recovering it was slim. Both sayings are recorded in Heywood's *A Dialogue conteyning Prouerbs and Epigrammes*, published in 1546.

to beard the lion

To be uncommonly and rashly brave; literally, to be so courageous as to dare to seize a lion by the beard. The saying is most familiar to us, perhaps, from the lines in Scott's *Marmion*:

> *. . . And dar'st thou then*
> *To beard the lion in his den,*
> *The Douglas in his hall?*
> *And hop'st thou thence unscathed*
> *to go?*
> *No, by St. Bryde of Bothwell, no!*

Scott was drawing upon a much older proverb, however, one cited by Shakespeare in *King John*, "You are the Hare of whom the Prouerb goes, Whose valour plucks dead Lyons by the Beard." Shakespeare quoted from Thomas Kyd's *The Spanish Tragedie*, perhaps—"Hares may pull dead lions by the beard." But the original source was undoubtedly the Latin saying, "Mortuo leoni et lepores insultant (And hares leaping at dead lions)."

by the skin of one's teeth

The use is always in respect to some calamity that has been avoided by so narrow a margin as to be measurable by the lining of a tooth. But originally, as found in Job xix, 20, the preposition "with" was used, not "by"—"And I am escaped with the skin of my teeth." But Job meant that he had escaped with nothing left but the skin of his teeth. The modern American expression and its meaning did not appear until approximately the beginning of the nineteenth century.

tarred with the same brush

The sense is always that of sharing, perhaps to a lesser degree, the faults or iniquities of another, of being defiled to some extent in the defilement of another. The record of usage goes back only to the late eighteenth century, though we may find its origin six centuries earlier. Early American usage, largely vanished now, alluded to a person of mixed blood; in Scotland the allusion was to sheep which had been smeared with tar as a protection against ticks. But it is likely that the real origin takes us back to the Crusades, to the introduction, in England at least, of the punishment, "tarring and feathering." This punishment could never have been humane, but when decreed by Richard the Lion-Hearted, in 1191, the chance of the survival of the victim must have been slight. A translation of that edict by Hakluyt, in 1589, reads, in part: "Concerning the lawes and ordinances appointed by King Richard for his navie the forme thereof was this . . . item, a thiefe or felon that hath stolen, being lawfully convicted, shal have his head shorne, and boyling pitch poured upon his head, and feathers or downe strawed upon the same whereby he may be knowen, and so at the first landing-place they shal come to, there to be cast up."

Through succeeding centuries tarring and feathering became a punishment for various misdemeanors inflicted, chiefly, by mobs. The nature of the punishment also varied. Rather than "boyling" pitch upon the shorn scalp, which must have horrible disfigured or killed the victim, the tar was heated enough to be viscid and was usually brushed, not poured, upon the scalp of the victim. Unless friendly hands and means were found to dissolve the tar, it would stay there a long time, for attempts to remove it otherwise would remove the skin with it. But when there was an accomplice of the chief victim, we may surmise that such a lesser rogue was punished less severely. Instead of hot tar and a pillowful of feathers, he may have received a swipe of the tarbrush and some of the feathers as a warning to mend his ways.

Tarring and feathering was not, of course, always applied only to the scalp. The culprits were often stripped, and both tar and feathers applied to the whole body. In frontier regions of the United States, as Mark Twain reminds us in *Huckleberry Finn*, villains thus treated by indignant townsmen might suffer the further indignity and torture of being set astride a rail, carried to the edge of the town, and warned against returning.

behind the eight ball

This modern expression has come to mean in a hazardous position; in a state or condition of embarrassment or peril from which it is difficult or impossible to extricate oneself; hence, out of luck; jinxed. The expression originated from the game of pocket billiards or, popularly, Kelly pool. But, though the origin seems to have been no

longer ago than about 1919 or 1920, there are already at least two versions of the manner in which the phrase assumed its meaning.

The popular version says that it comes from a variant of the game of Kelly pool in which the players must pocket all fifteen balls, except that numbered "eight," in numerical order. But the eight ball, which is usually colored black, is considered unlucky, and if a player in the course of his shots has the misfortune to hit or touch the eight ball with the cue ball, he is penalized. Thus if, during the play, the cue ball comes to rest on such a spot that the eight ball lies between the next ball to be played, the player may be faced with an impossible shot or one that can be made only by skilful cushion shots.

Such a game as that just described is played, and it is easy to see that "behind the eight ball" would come to mean a hazardous position. But there is very good reason to believe that the phrase came first; that this variant of Kelly pool was a later development, making use of the phrase to introduce a new element of difficulty in the regular game.

The real story of the phrase, according to Charles C. Peterson, the noted billiardist, is that it originated in 1919 in a billiard room on John Street, New York, where a group of businessmen met each noon for a game of Kelly pool. In this game each player draws a number, and, if there are more than eight players, a player drawing a number higher than eight has no possible chance of winning. In this group of players, according to Peterson, "One player, time after time, day after day, would shake a number higher than eight. This became especially trying, because the group always placed side bets on lucky numbers under eight. One day when the 'pot' was extra interesting this player got an unusually high number. With a roar he threw it down and bellowed, 'I never have any luck! I'm always behind that doggoned ! ! * * ! ! eight ball!' "

Peterson says that the expression was first brought to his attention during a championship billiard tournament at the Hotel Astor, New York, in 1920, when Hoppe, Schaefer, and Cochran were contesting. He heard the full story in 1933 from Otto Reiselt, of Philadelphia, who gave the name of the unlucky originator of the expression as Allie Flint.

to stew in one's own juice

To suffer the consequences of one's own act. This, or its variant, "to fry in one's own grease," is very old. In the latter form it appears in a thirteenth-century tale of Richard the Lion-Hearted, and there is a French equivalent, *cuire dans son jus*. It is presumable that the older expression, at least, was originally literal; one fried in his own grease who, having committed some act punishable by such means, was burned at the stake.

to laugh in one's sleeve

To be secretly amused, whether in derision or just to avoid offense through open laughter, is to laugh in one's sleeve. The saying dates from the first half of the sixteenth century when, as one would suppose, the sleeves of a gentleman's costume were distinctly over-size, large enough to conceal one's whole head, let alone the mouth. The French, at the same period and earlier, laughed in their capes, which were large and flowing; and the Spaniard could conceal his amusement by laughing in his beard.

Bronx cheer

This somewhat disgusting sound expressing contemptuous dis-approval, the reverse of a cheer—a vibrating sound partly uttered through loosely closed lips and partly through the nose—seemingly owes its present name to the unusual skill displayed by the residents of the northern geographical section of New York City, or to spec-tators at athletic sports events held in that borough, in loudly producing this vocal effect. Before, roughly, a dozen years ago, the same sound was called "the raspberry," usually written "razz-berry"; to "get the raspberry," or "to give one the raspberry" was in slang use as early as the 1890s and is still regarded as a more refined expression than "Bronx cheer," if refinement may be considered in this con-nection. "Raspberry" was and is frequently shortened to "the berries." The British equivalent is "to get, or to give (one) the bird," a usage that traces back to theatrical slang of the middle nineteenth century.

It has been gravely suggested that the use of "raspberry" as the name of the sound arose from the resemblance to the noise pro-duced by a rasp grated over metal. I don't think so. I think that the word should be written "razzberry," that it was a humorous exten-sion developed from the slang, "to razz," to mock at or make fun of"; and that the latter term was originally a contraction of "to razzle-dazzle," meaning to bamboozle, banter, or deceive. And this latter verb, it may be recalled, came from the American invention in the 1880s of the razzle-dazzle, a kind of merry-go-round with an undulating platform, thus giving its passengers the combined pleasures of dizziness and seasickness.

to knock (something) galley-west

Aunt Sally, if you remember *Huckleberry Finn*, got so upset when trying to count the silver spoons—sometimes making a count of nine, sometimes ten, thanks to Huck's manipulations—that she seized the spoon basket, slammed it across the room, and knocked the cat "galley-west." It means that the cat was knocked upside down, topsy-turvy, into a state of confusion. Mark Twain's use happens to be the first on record, and one would almost expect to learn that he had coined the expression. Perhaps he did, but it is more likely that he heard it from someone else, either during the years that he was a pilot on the Mississippi or during the time he spent in western mining camps, for the term was already fairly common when, in 1882, he wrote *Huckleberry Finn*.

In fact, it is reasonably certain that the American "galley-west" is a corruption of the dialectal English "collyweston." This, used with much the same meaning—askew, awry, confused—has been traced by C. L. Apperson to 1587, and may be much earlier. The ultimate source is not known, but may have come from the name or nickname of an individual. In some English counties, there has long been a saying, "It's all along o' Colly Weston," used when anything has gone wrong. But whether "Colly Weston" was ever an actual person or just the name of a mischievous elf, like Robin Goodfellow, is not on the records.

another county heard from

Someone who has listened to—but has taken no part in—a debate or argument, finally breaks his silence. "Another county heard from," someone else is sure to remark brightly. The allusion is to the presidential election of 1876; Tilden and Hayes had had a neck-and-neck campaign; neither the Democrats nor the Republicans had been overscrupulous, and the results of the election were in grave doubt. Tilden, Democratic nominee, was believed to have carried all the southern states, but on the day after the election, word was sent out from the Republican headquarters that Hayes had carried Florida, Louisiana, and South Carolina. A recount of the ballots was ordered and, during the next several months, the suspense was high. Tallies from the various counties were so slow that as each came in a wearied public ironically remarked, "Another county heard from."

to skin the cat

In America, as any country boy knows, this means to hang by the hands from a branch or bar, draw the legs up through the arms and  over the branch, and pull oneself up into a sitting position. As we must abide by the record, we cannot say positively that the name for this violent small-boy exercise is more than a century old, but it is highly likely that Ben Franklin or earlier American lads had the same name for it. No one got around to putting it into print until about 1845. One can't be certain why the operation was called "skinning the cat," but maybe some mother, seeing it for the first time, saw in it some resemblance to the physical operation of removing the pelt from a cat, first from the forelegs and down over the body.

pieces of eight

This expression intrigued me as a youngster; it turned up in all the yarns about the Spanish Main, but was so obscure. Eight what? Actually, there was nothing mysterious about it, the term was merely the plural of the Spanish dollar which, having the value of eight reals, was stamped with a large figure 8. Until as late as our War Between the States the Spanish dollar was in general circulation in the United States, its value being almost the same as the United States dollar. It was from the Spanish dollar, or piece-of-eight, that we have our fictitious unit, the "bit," valued artificially at twelve and a half cents. The bit is, of course, the real, or one eighth of the dollar; "two bits" is twenty-five cents; "four bits" is fifty cents.

to draw (or pull) in one's horns

The use of this figure of speech with the meaning, "to retract, or to check oneself," has been traced back to the fourteenth century.

The allusion is to the snail which, when its hornlike tentacles touch something strange, possibly perilous, immediately retracts one or both of them.

iron curtain

Not often is a phrase, coined for a particular occasion, immediately seized upon, and widely used. This phrase, however, so aptly described a condition which was disturbing half the globe that it achieved immediate popularity. It was coined by Winston Churchill who, as prime minister of Great Britain during World War II, had an unequaled view of European politics during those critical years. The rise of Russian influence over eastern Europe disturbed him, accompanied as it was by rigid censorship and closed borders. When, no longer prime minister, he visited the United States in 1946, he felt free to express his misgivings. In a speech on March 5 at Fulton, Mo., where he was receiving an honorary degree from Westminster College, he expressed his concern in the following words:

From Stettin in the Baltic to Trieste in the Adriatic, an iron curtain has descended across the continent. Behind that line lie all the capitals of the ancient states of central and eastern Europe. Warsaw, Berlin, Prague, Vienna, Budapest, Belgrade, Bucharest, and Sofia, all these famous cities and the populations around them lie in what I might call the Soviet sphere, and all are subject, in one form or another, not only to Soviet influence but to a very high and in some cases increasing measure of control from Moscow.

to return to one's muttons

The English saying is a direct translation from the French, *revenon à nos moutons*. The literal meaning in the French phrase is the same as the English, and the figurative meanings are also the same— to return to the subject under discussion or consideration. For the origin we must go to a sixteenth-century play, *Pierre Pathelin*, written by the French poet, Pierre Blanchet. Pathelin (often spelled Patelin) is a lawyer who has, through flattery, hoodwinked Joceaume, the local draper, into giving him six ells of cloth. While this injury is still rankling, Joceaume also discovers that his shepherd has stolen some of his sheep. He has the shepherd haled before the magistrate and there finds to his amazement that the shepherd has the rascally Pathelin as his lawyer. The draper, sputtering in indignation, tries to tell the magistrate about his loss of the sheep, but each time that he sees Pathelin he begins to rave about the cloth of which he has been defrauded. The judge begins to get somewhat confused, but tries to keep Joceaume to his charges against the shepherd: "Revenon à nos moutons (Let us return to our sheep)," he repeats time and again.

to have bees in one's bonnet

To be slightly daft or crazed. The original saying, which dates at least to the sixteenth century was, "to have a head full of bees," or "to have bees in the head, or in the brain." That association of

craziness with bees humming in the head undoubtedly antedates that period, for the expression is recorded by John Heywood, in 1546, in his *Dialogue conteining the nomber in effect of all the prouerbes in the Englishe tongue,* though no earlier quotation has been found. According to Apperson, the poet, Robert Herrick was the person who introduced the bonnet into the expression. This was found in Herrick's "Mad Maid's Song," written in 1648: "Ah! woe is mee, woe, woe is mee, Alack and well-a-day! For pitty, sir, find out that bee, Which bore my love away. I'le seek him in your bonnet brave, I'le seek him in your eyes."

just under the wire

One who no more than barely catches a train, who has hardly settled himself in a theater seat before the curtain rises, who in a moment more would have been too late for whatever the event might be, is said to be "just under the wire." The expression comes from the racetracks. The winning horse is the first to go "under the wire"—the "wire" being a figment of the imagination, but denoting the exact line that marks the finish of a race. But in many races, though the winning horse receives the major part of the purse, the second, third, and often the fourth horses are also "in the money"—that is, receive a share of the prize. Thus a horse that just noses ahead of the fourth (or sometimes fifth) horse to cross the finish line is "just under the wire."

to sow one's wild oats

To indulge in dissipation, or to conduct oneself foolishly. The saying has been common in its present sense for at least four hundred years, for a writer of that period speaks of young men at "that wilfull and unruly age, which lacketh rypenes and discretion, and (as wee saye) hath not sowed all theyr wyeld Oates." The reference is to a genus of cereal grass, known as wild oat (*Avena fatua*), that flourishes throughout Europe. It is little more than  a weed and is very difficult to eradicate. The folly of sowing it is comparable to the folly shown by young men who, thoughtlessly, commit an act or begin a practice the evil of which will be difficult to eradicate.

I'm from Missouri

In America, extreme skepticism is indicated by one who says, "I'm from Missouri," though actually the residents of that state are no more incredulous than are other Americans. The expression is said to have originated during the course of some extemporaneous humorous remarks by Willard D. Vandiver who was, at the time, a representative to Congress from Missouri. The occasion, according to the Washington *Post*, May 31, 1932, was an impromptu address before the Five O'clock Club of Philadelphia in 1899. The previous speaker had made some extravagant assertions, it was said, for the productiveness of the prosperous state of Iowa. In casting doubt on some of those statements, Vandiver said, "I come from a country that raises corn, cotton, cockleburs, and Democrats. I'm from

Missouri, and you've got to show me." The implication of hard-headedness and shrewdness immediately appealed to the natives of Missouri, and especially the last part of their congressman's statement, and it was not long before they began to call themselves citizens of the "Show Me" state—and for all others, when some speaker drew the longbow, to smile and say, "I'm from Missouri."

the whole kit and caboodle

In its entirety, this phrase is American; it is a somewhat more refined expression than the earlier, "the whole kit and bilin'." Both forms mean lock, stock, and barrel; the whole lot, omitting nothing. But "the whole kit" is plain English—the entire outfit; the whole lot, either of things or persons. "Bilin'," of course, was corrupted from "boiling," which meant a seething mass, especially of persons; so "the whole kit and bilin' " originally meant the entire group of people and their equipment. Later it was limited to define just all the people in a group.

But along with the common expression, "the whole kit and bilin'," there was a more refined American phrase, "the whole kit and boodle," for "boodle" was apparently Americanized from the Dutch word *boedel*, property, estate, goods. And just because we like to have alliteration in our speech, someone tried to put a "*k*" before "boodle," giving us, "the whole kit and caboodle." By the way, it was this same Dutch word, corrupted to "boodle" also, that was later used in a sinister sense to mean money—money acquired by graft or bribery.

holding the bag (or *sack*)

We saw elsewhere how "to let the cat out of the bag" was connected with the other familiar saying, "to buy a pig in a poke." Proof is lacking, but it seems to me that the unfortunate wight who bought a pig in a poke and soon after let a cat out of the bag, could very well have served as the prototype of the person who was left holding the bag. This saying is also old, and from its first appearance in literature has meant "left in the lurch," holding responsibilities that one has not contracted which have been evaded by the one who should bear them.

balled up

This has been used, in the sense of confused, embarrassed, entangled, only since about 1880, if we allow seven or eight years of that puristic period for a slang expression to break into print. Really, however, the slang use is little more than a natural extension of the normal use of the verb, "to ball," which is to form or to be formed into a ball—one balls a hank of yarn, for instance. But our phrase does not come so much from the state that grandma's knitting yarn sometimes got into, as from grandpa's horses. When driven during spring thaws or over soft winter snows, the snow often  became packed into rounded icy balls on the hoofs of the horses; it became "balled" or "balled up." Not only was progress difficult, but sometimes the horses were unable to keep their footing. When they fell, either singly or in pairs, the state of confusion and entanglement was exasperating, giving rise to the present use of the expression.

to pass the buck

There is no uncertainty about the source of this term. Poker. But, just as the origin of the American game of poker is shrouded in mystery, so is the origin of this phrase. Probably both the name of the game and the game itself come from an old German game, *pochspiel*, which was also a game of bluff, but this is little more than a guess. The game seems to have developed in the United States during the first quarter of the nineteenth century; first as straight poker, and later, about 1845, with draw poker its earliest modification. Until comparatively recent years, poker was not what would have been called a "gentlemen's game"; it was a game for the barroom or for the lumber or mining camp. Few of the men who played it were literate, and, therefore, the reasons or the occasions for some of the terms used in the game were not recorded. No one knows, for instance, how "stud poker" got its name. It may be, as someone has surmised, that a stud horse was the stake in an early exciting stage of its development. Our present phrase, "to pass the buck," came into use probably around the time of the Civil War, though Mark Twain, in 1872, gives us the earliest record of it. The "buck" was some sort of object passed from one player to another as a reminder that the next deal would fall to the second person. Because of the present-day practice of using a pocket knife for the purpose, and because early knives often had buckhorn handles, it has been suggested that "buck" came from that source. That is possible, but, in my opinion, unlikely. Knives carried by the poker players of that period were more likely to be hunting knives than pocket knives, and were too large for so slight a purpose. A buckshot would have served the need, or, possibly, a bucktail carried as a talisman.

bats in one's belfry

One wonders why such a typical Americanism was not coined until early in the present century. I suspect that it must have come  from the fertile imagination of Sime Silverman, the editorial genius and apt word-coiner who guided the theatrical journal, *Variety*, until his death in 1933, but if so, I find no proof. The earliest record is in 1911, in a novel by Henry Sydnor Harrison. Even the derivative, "batty," a slang equivalent for crazy, was a later development. The explanation is simple: as "belfry" is that part of a church tower in which the bells are hung, it suggests, therefore, the head. Bats are known to be frequenters of bell towers; they fly around crazily; ergo, they are crazy. Hence, to have bats in one's belfry is to be crazy in the head.

to put in one's best licks

Through some queer chance, the word "lick" in American speech acquired the meaning "a spurt of speed; also, a burst of energy."

This meaning found its way into print early in the nineteenth century. Our present phrase was derived from that sense and is graphically illustrated by the line from *Polly Peablossom's Wedding*, published in 1851 by T. A. Burke. The line reads, "I saw comin' my gray mule, puttin' in her best licks, and a few yards behind her was a grizzly." We also say, to put in "solid" licks, or "good" licks.

Annie Oakley

In theater or show parlance, an "Annie Oakley" is a free pass to the show. The real Annie Oakley, born in 1860, was an expert American markswoman. During the years when William F. Cody, perhaps better known as "Buffalo Bill," was touring the country with his Wild West Show, organized in 1883, one of his stellar attractions from 1885 to 1902 was this marvelous markswoman. Her full name was Phoebe Anne Oakley Mozes; she was not a "westerner" at all, but hailed from Ohio; her husband, whom she married at the age of fifteen, was Frank Butler, a vaudeville actor. Her marksmanship was exceptional; her most notable achievement, it is said, was by 1000 shots with a rifle to break 942 glass balls tossed in the air. In the Wild West Show a playing card, such as the ten of diamonds, was pinned to a target and, in successive shots, she would center a shot in each one of the pips. It was through this latter accomplishment that her name became synonymous with a complimentary pass to a show, because the card, when thus perforated, resembled a theater ticket which the manager has punched before issuing it as a pass.

to come to the end of one's rope (or *tether*)

"Tether" is the older word, but with either "rope" or "tether" the saying goes back many centuries. In original usage the expression alluded apparently to a cow or other domestic animal, perchance a dog, staked for grazing or for protection by a rope attached to its neck. The range of the animal was thus limited. If a cow, it could not graze beyond the limit of its rope; if a dog, it could not get at a stranger, no matter how fiercely it might run or lunge, who kept outside the circle of its tether. Thus, "to come to the end of one's rope" had the literal meaning, to reach the limit of one's resources.

But both rope and tether early became sinister synonyms for the hangman's rope. From this, the saying acquired a second and more devastating meaning by which we use it to signify that one has been effectually checked in the commission of crime, has reached, figuratively, if not literally, the noose of the hangman. It is probable that this extended meaning was effected, in part at least, by the old proverb, "Give him enough rope and he'll hang himself."

to lay an egg

This modern slang expression has no bearing whatsoever upon the output of a hen. It means, "to fail; to flop; to fail to produce an intended result." The "egg" in the expression is shortened from the older slang meaning of "goose-egg," which, in sporting circles, means a cipher, a nought, a zero, from the resemblance of the outline of the egg to a cipher, o. In an inning of baseball, for example, the score of a team which has no runs is shown by the figure o, a cipher. That team "lays an egg."

"Goose-egg" in this sense had attained some degree of respectability by 1886, for in that year it is recorded that the New York *Times*, in reporting a baseball game, said, "The New York players presented the Boston men with nine unpalatable goose eggs in their contest on the Polo Grounds yesterday." The American usage, however, is merely a transference from the British "duck" as the layer of such eggs, for, as readers of Charles Reade's *Hard Cash* will discover, as long ago as 1863 and earlier, the British were describing one who failed to score at cricket as having "achieved a duck's egg." Sports writers of today leave the bird nameless.

the spit an' image

Though spelled and contracted in different ways—spit and image, spitting image, spittin' image, spitten image—the intent is always the same, an exact likeness, a counterpart. It usually refers to an infant or child whose features and mannerisms strongly reflect those of one of its parents. The origin of the expression has been variously ascribed; thus, for example, the late O. O. McIntyre, newspaper columnist, offered the ingenious suggestion that it may have been an American Negro corruption of "spirit and image," that the child possessed the spirit and was the image of its parent.

In my opinion, however, the expression is partly English and partly American. The records show that "spit," in such form as "the spit of his father," was used in England early in the nineteenth century. It seems certain that the origin of the noun in this sense was derived from an earlier use of the verb, going back over some two hundred years, for earlier records show such expressions as, "as like (a person or animal) as if spit out of his mouth."

"Image" seems to have been a redundancy added in America. It was not needed, and only serves to intensify the close resemblance which the speaker observes. Records do not show that the doubled term was in use much before the middle of the past century.

to turn the heat on

This seems originally to have been underworld slang, probably a rough interpretation of "to be grilled" in its figurative sense. It means, to be subjected to a severe cross-examination, as by police officers in grilling a suspected criminal; but of course in ordinary use a youngster will say that his dad turned the heat on when asking how the fender of the car got dented. The expression is quite recent.

to be hand in glove

To be on such terms of intimacy that the relationship is almost that of the glove to the hand. Literary usage dates back to 1678, but in those days and until late in the following century the phrase was "hand and glove," a form rarely heard nowadays.

white elephant

That large portrait of your wealthy Aunt Jane, given by her and which you loathe but do not dare to take down from your wall; that large bookcase, too costly to discard, but which you hope will be more in keeping with your future home; these, and a thousand other like items are "white elephants"—costly, but useless possessions. The allusion takes us to Siam.

In that country it was the traditional custom for many centuries that a rare albino elephant was, upon capture, the property of the emperor—who even today bears the title, Lord of the White Elephant—and was thereafter sacred to him. He alone might ride or use such an animal, and none might be destroyed without his consent. Because of that latter royal prerogative, it is said that whenever it pleased his gracious majesty to bring about the ruin of a courtier who had displeased him, he would present the poor fellow with an elephant from his stables. The cost of feeding and caring for the huge animal that he might not use nor destroy—a veritable white elephant—gave the term its present meaning.

Incidentally, as a matter of English history, Charles I of England had the sad experience of receiving such a gift, a figurative, if not literal, white elephant. In 1629, just at the time that the king, faced with a recalcitrant Parliament, was desperately trying to raise funds by any measures, even to the extent of bartering the crown jewels, the Emperor of Siam sent him an elephant and five camels. Though the account does not say that the elephant was white, the cost of keeping the beast, estimated at £275 a year, was so great that the queen was obliged to put off her "visit to 'the Bath' to a more convenient season, for want of money to bear her charges," for, as the record goes on to say, aside from that cost for feed and care, "his keepers afirme that from the month of September until April he must drink, not water, but wyne, and from April unto September he must have a gallon of wyne the daye."

to swallow (a tale) hook, line, and sinker

We use this saying of a person so exceedingly gullible as to accept a yarn or statement, no matter how fantastic, at its face value. The allusion is to a hungry fish, so voracious as to take into its maw not only the baited fish hook, but the leaden sinker and all the line between, thus falling an easy prey to the fisherman. It is an American expression and, though undoubtedly long and widely used earlier, was first recorded in the course of a congressional debate in 1865. There was a British antecedent, however, that had the same meaning and a similar piscatorial background—to swallow a gudgeon. This goes back to the sixteenth century at least, used by John Lyly in his romance, *Euphues*, in 1579. And a later writer, still in the sixteenth century, spoke of one who had swallowed the gudgeon and had been entangled in the hook. A gudgeon, incidentally, is a small fish often used as bait, a minnow.

to come out at the little end of the horn

To fail in an undertaking; especially, to fail after one has bragged about a result that promised large returns. Such has been the meaning of this expression for more than three hundred years. From the statement made by John Fletcher, in *A Wife for a Month* (1625)—"the prodigal fool the ballad speaks of, that was squeezed through a horn" —it appears that the saying arose from some old popular ballad, one that has not survived. But the allusion has come to us through other channels. George Chapman, in *Eastward Hoe!* written in collaboration with Jonson and Marston (1605), says, "I had the Horne of Suretiship ever before my eyes. You all know the deuise of the  Horne, where the young fellow slippes in at the Butte end, and comes squesd out at the Buckall." And a correspondent to *Notes & Queries* (Seventh Series) described an old painting ascribed to the sixteenth century that he had seen, on which was depicted a huge horn into which a man had been thrust, the head and arms emerging from the small end; underneath were the lines:

This horne emblem here doth show
Of svretishipp what harm doth grow.

From these we can surmise that the lost ballad probably related the sad experience of a young man who, coming into a fortune, accepted bad advice in the handling of it. It would appear that, under the promise of handsome dividends, he became surety for a false friend and, having to pay the obligation, lost all his heritage in the bitter experience. The moral probably pointed to the ease with which money can be lent, like entering the mouth of a horn, but the lender may find himself squeezed and stripped when promises are not fulfilled.

not amount to Hannah More

This saying, equivalent to "not amount to a hill of beans," is a common way of telling a young person around Gloucester, Massachusetts, that he doesn't show much promise. The saying was also current in some parts of England many years ago, but why the name of Miss Hannah More became bandied about in such manner is a mystery. Hannah More, born near Bristol, England, in 1745, the daughter of a boarding-school master, began to write while still in her teens, and to have those writings published. A friend of the actor, Garrick, she wrote two slightly successful tragedies. But before she was thirty her work turned to moral and religious topics and, in 1795, one of these, *Cheap Repository Tracts*, had such success that two million copies of it were circulated in its first year. In 1809 her most successful work, *Coelebs in Search of a Wife*, which despite its title was a religious novel, reached the remarkable sale, for that period, of ten editions in its first year. It was very popular, also, in the United States. She died at the ripe age of eighty-eight after a long bedridden period during which she produced a half-dozen or so other serious works. After such a notable career, it is odd that her name ever became a word of disparagement. The suggestion has been offered that, despite her assiduous work, nothing ever came of it; but if that be the interpretation, thousands of other names might be infinitely more appropriate.

to beat the Dutch

Though "Dutch courage" as a synonym for sham courage and "Dutch consolation" as a synomym for "Well, it might be worse," date back to the days of rivalry in arms and commerce between the countries of Holland and England, "to beat the Dutch" is traceable only to late American colonial days. Under English rule of New York descendants of the early Dutch settlers became successful merchants and traders, just as their forefathers as citizens of New Amsterdam had been. They dealt in good wares which they offered at fair prices, and he who would excel any of these merchants had good reason to boast that he had, literally, beat the Dutch. From that early literal meaning the phrase became a popular expression used to denote surprise or wonderment, and often interchangeable with "to beat the band." In the presidential campaign of Martin Van Buren his Dutch ancestry was used against him in a popular song that ran:

> *We'll beat the Dutch,*
> *Hurrah for Tyler!*
> *We'll beat the Dutch,*
> *Or bust our b'iler.*

a fig for your opinion, not worth a fig, not to care a fig

These sayings, which express contempt, may go back to ancient Greece, to a region where figs were so plentiful as to have almost no value. But more probably we got the worthlessness of a fig from Italy, where a gesture—the thumb thrust between the fingers—said to have an indecent significance, is called a "fig" and has been for many centuries expressive of the deepest contempt. It is interesting to note that English writers of the sixteenth century referred to this gesture as "a fig of Spain."

The Italian source is said to have originated in the twelfth century, as the result of an event in Milan. The citizens of that proud city, resenting its seizure by Frederick Barbarossa in 1158, overthrew its conqueror in 1159 and drove him from the city. His empress, in derision, was placed upon a mule, facing its tail, and escorted outside the city walls. But in 1162 Frederick recaptured Milan, razed its buildings, and humiliated its citizens. Those who were taken prisoners were compelled, on pain of death, to take a "fig"—in the slang of that day, the droppings of a mule—between his teeth and to repeat to his captors, "Ecco la fica, (Behold the fig)."

a wolf in sheep's clothing

Young people of today think they are very up to date when they refer to a carnally minded man, young or old, as a "wolf," but the fact is that they are, roughly speaking, some twenty-five hundred years behind the times. So anciently were such men known that Aesop, who lived in Greece about 600 B.C., told a fable about them.

 He likened them to a wolf who got admission into a sheepfold by wrapping himself in the skin and fleece of a sheep. Thus, under the pretense that he was an innocent and harmless as a sheep, he was able to seize and devour unsuspecting young lambs that took his fancy.

The fables of Aesop were so familiar in Greece and the countries with which she enjoyed commerce that, possibly, this fable may have been the source of the passage in Matthew vii, 15: "Beware of false prophets, which come to you in sheep's clothing, but inwardly they are ravening wolves." Or, perhaps, today's ravening "wolf" got his name from the biblical passage, rather than directly from the fable, though no one can be certain.

to grin like a Cheshire cat

Lewis Carrol popularized the Cheshire cat in *Alice's Adventures in Wonderland*, in which the grinning cat disappeared gradually from Alice's view and the last to vanish was the grin, but the saying is much older than this account. It has been traced back to the writings of John Wolcot, better known under his pseudonym, Peter Pindar, whose numerous satires appeared between 1782 and 1819. But the saying must have originated some time before Wolcot's use, for by 1850, when people began to be interested in seeking its allusion, no grandsire or grandam could be found who had positive knowledge. One novel opinion was that, because Cheshire was a county palatine—that is, had regal privileges—the cats, when they thought of it, were so tickled that they couldn't help grinning. But the most likely opinion was that some influential family in Cheshire, with a lion rampant as its crest, employed some sign painter to paint the crest on the signboards of many of the inns. The painter was none too sure of the appearance of a lion and the final result looked, to the countryfolk, like an attempt to depict a grinning cat.

to stick one's neck out

When you vounteer for something that may have a bad ending, when you enter an argument in which you may turn out to be a poor second, or whenever you deliberately take the chance of being hurt, literally or figuratively, you are sticking your neck out. The saying is modern American slang, an outgrowth of the earlier, "to get it in the neck," both of them alluding to the neck of a chicken stretched for the ax. The other saying attained popularity during the last quarter of the nineteenth century.

to carry the torch for one

It is the torch of love that is understood in this modern American term, though sometimes no more than the torch of loyalty, for the "torchbearer" is one who is loud in his praise of a friend. But the torch has long been an emblem of enlightenment and of burning devotion, and, in 1775, Richard Sheridan used the expression, "The torch of love," in his epilog to *The Rivals*.

rope of sand

Nothing could be less cohesive or less stable. With just such meaning the expression has been used through the past three hundred and fifty years, ironically describing a treaty, contract, or the like which has no force, as a "rope of sand" binding the two parties. As used by Sir Francis Bacon and other sixteenth-century writers, one was supposed "to knit a rope of sand." Samuel Butler, the satirist, wrote in 1712, "I leave to my said children a great chest full of broken promises and cracked oaths; likewise a vast cargo of ropes made with sand."

to make one's mouth water

To anticipate something with great eagerness. Literally, and the original sense, one referred to the actual drooling that one experiences over the prospects of sinking one's teeth into a comestible that exudes a particularly delightful aroma, as a schoolboy from Boston might say. The experience must have been as early as mankind, but  it may be that early English cooking occasioned no such outpouring of saliva, for it was not until 1555 that the saying appeared in English print, and then in reference to some West Indian cannibals. The historian, Richard Eden, in *The Decades of the Newe Worlde or West India,* wrote, "These craftie foxes . . . espying their enemies afarre of, beganne to swalowe theyr spettle as their mouthes watered for greedines of theyr pray."

worth one's salt; to earn one's salt

We may as well take these together, for it is only the use of "salt" in these phrases that is interesting. Because of the origin of the word, one would expect to be able to find that either of the expressions could be traced to ancient Latin, but actually the first of them, the earliest, goes back only to the first quarter of the nineteenth century. "Salt," in these expressions, is no more than an etymological play upon the source of the word "salary," perhaps a source that was not understood before 1800. In the days of the Roman legions, a soldier received a part of his pay in the form of a *salarium,* a salary, which was actually an allowance for the purchase of salt (Latin, *sal*). Salt was not so easily obtainable in those times, but even then the Roman generals knew that this mineral was essential to health and vigor. A soldier who was not worth or did not earn this small allowance was worthless indeed.

to beat the band

This saying has become so trite as to be employed for almost any element of amazement or of any superior accomplishment or achievement; as, Well, if that doesn't beat the band! or, She cooks to beat the band; or, The baby yelled to beat the band. The expression isn't very old; at least, no literary record of it has been dug up earlier than fifty years ago, but, probably because of its enticing alliteration, it has acquired great general use in the United States. Its origin seems to have been literal, a desire to arrive at some spot before a band of musicians leading a parade had passed that spot, thereby enabling one to see the entire parade. Sometimes one had to whip up one's horses to get there, or, if a small boy, run on the wings of the wind, but the later pleasure made the haste worth while.

to jump the gun

This expression is of racing origin, especially foot racing. A contestant so keyed up as to spring from the starting mark a moment before the starter fires his pistol is said "to jump the gun." The expression is also used in hunting game, as when a pheasant "jumps the gun" by being startled and taking flight before the sportsman's gun is in readiness. Hence, the phrase has acquired a general slang meaning of beginning a thing before preparations for  it are in readiness. In this figurative sense the usage is recent, probably not longer than within the past twenty-five or thirty years.

to stab in the back

We use this now always figuratively, to deliver a cowardly blow, physically or against one's character, and we usually use it with reference to such a delivery by one who was thought to be friendly, or at least not suspected to be inimical. The literal origin goes back to the times when footpads, with a dagger beneath the cape, would unconcernedly approach and pass an unsuspecting victim, quickly flash out the knife as the pedestrian was passing and thrust it into his back, grabbing his purse as he fell, and dashing away from the scene.

to take the cake

To receive or merit a prize or honor; hence, to excel at something. This expression did not arise from the "cakewalk," but the cakewalk got its name from the expression. Even two hundred years ago "cake" denoted an award or honor of some sort, and he who received it, "took the cake." American usage can be traced back a hundred years. The cakewalk, originally a Negro entertainment in which couples competed for a cake by the grace or style of walking, came into notice only in the last quarter of the nineteenth century.

to shoot the bull

This American slang, which originated in the gutter or, rather, the barnyard, now means to talk pretentiously, to talk wisely and freely upon subjects about which one knows little. It developed from the American institution known as a "bull session," a gathering of men, usually young men, in which each airs his knowledge or offers his opinions upon any subject toward which the conversation, often smutty, veers. "Bull" in each instance refers generically to a type of commodity, known euphemistically as "booshwah," found abundantly upon cattle farms, which forms a cheap fertilizer and reeks unpleasantly. Both "bull session" and "to shoot the bull" are developments of the twentieth century.

crocodile tears

It is proverbial that a crocodile moans and sobs like a person in great distress in order to lure a man into its reach, and then, after devouring him sheds bitter tears over the dire fate of its victim. Thus "crocodile tears" is synonymous with hypocritical grief, make-believe deep sorrow. Belief in the proverb is found in ancient Greek and Latin literature, so it was natural that untraveled Englishmen, to whom a crocodile was unknown, accepted the belief as a statement of fact in early days. In the *Voiage and Travaile of Sir John Maundeville*, written about 1400, we read that "Cokadrilles. . . . Theise Serpentes slen men, and thei eten hem wepynge." Other English writers repeated the fable, and we find it even in Shakespeare's works.

going to town

Usually in our jocular use of this phrase we slur it to "goin' to town." It means alert and eager, full of life and vivacity, in the state or condition in which Fortune shines upon one. Although a very modern expression, we must seek its significance in the backwoods days of more than half a century ago when, for many persons, a visit to a town was a momentous event. One prepared several days in advance for such a trip, getting one's clothes in order and making up a shopping list.  The trip and the visit itself were filled with interest. The occasion, if the weather were fine, was one of great good fortune. In modern usage the phrase retains much of that same spirit of high adventure.

out on a limb

At a disadvantage, as one would be if actually upon the limb of a tree, hanging on for dear life and being pelted or shot at by an enemy. The expression is of American origin and dates from the latter part of the nineteenth century. Its earliest literary appearance was, in 1897, by Alfred Henry Lewis who, under the pen name of Dan Quin, wrote *Wolfville*, one of a series of tales about life in a frontier town.

to get the brush-off

If your employer dismisses you, or if your boy friend ceases to call, or if the newcomer on the next street rejects your friendly advances, you are—in modern American slang—getting the brush-off; you are being put aside. The thought seems to be that one is likened to an undesirable piece of lint or streak of dirt that is brushed from a garment. But there is also the possibility that the allusion is to a Pullman porter who, sensing a poor tip from one of his charges, gives that person a few flicks with his brush and passes on to a more likely customer.

to give a lick and a promise

If small Johnny has taken the facecloth and lightly washed his mouth and cheeks, he has given himself a lick and a promise—about what the cat could do in one hasty swab of the tongue and a promise of a complete job in the dim future. We say that one who has worked half-heartedly or in a slovenly manner has given the work a lick and a promise. The homely saying is common in both England and America; it is undoubtedly several centuries old, but examples of literary use are not recorded.

to chew the rag

To talk, or to make a speech; especially, to talk at length, to grumble continuously, or to rant. As with any slang expression, the parentage and time of birth of this cannot be positively determined. Records of written use are simultaneous in England and the United States, in 1885—army slang in England, newspaper use in this country; so it is certain that the man in the street of either country had been using the expression a long time before that. But this noun, rag, I think, never had any connection with the ordinary rag, a strip of cloth. It seems to have been formed from the verb, to rag—which, in dialectal English back in the eighteenth century, meant, to scold; hence, to annoy, tease; also, to wrangle. No one knows the source of this "rag," but it is supposed to have been a contraction of "bully-rag."

As to chewing, in this figurative sense pertaining to words, we can find that use in Shakespeare. In *Measure for Measure*, he has Angelo chewing a name; that is, saying it over and over. And away back in the sixteenth century, the expression, "to chew the cud," meaning to ruminate upon a matter, was already proverbial.

to have a bone to pick

The bone, originally, was a bone of contention—some difference of opinion to argue about or to settle, thus resembling an actual bone tossed between two dogs to determine which should be the master. One has a bone to pick with one when one has an argument to settle or something disagreeable to discuss or have explained. Usage goes back to the middle of the sixteenth century, but the expression may well have been derived from, or another form of, the earlier phrase, "to have a crow to pluck," which was used at least a hundred years earlier, but for which no satisfactory explanation has been discovered.

sword of Damocles

When Dionysius was ruler of Syracuse, back in the fourth century B.C., the courtier, Damocles, wishing to curry favor, began to praise the ruler one day. He exclaimed over the power that Dionysius wielded, extolled his great wealth, and admired, above all, the luxurious life that he led and the comfort with which he was surrounded. Dionysius, it is said, began to grow somewhat weary of this fulsome flattery, and asked the courtier if he would himself like to experience such a life. Naturally, Damocles would like nothing better. So the ruler ordered that a bath should be prepared for Damocles, that he be arrayed in fine raiment, that a feast be set before him, and that dancers and singers should entertain him while he ate. All this was done, and when Damocles had finished his sumptuous repast he lay back on the couch upon which he had been reclining, and was aghast to see over his head a heavy sword, hanging by a single hair. He jumped from the couch, asking the meaning of so ominous a threat. "That," said Dionysius, "is the threat of calamity that always imperils the life of anyone in high position, for others are always seeking his downfall." The story is told by various ancient writers, but the simile, expressing imminent danger, was not employed in English literature until a scant two hundred years ago.

to do (or pull) a brodie

This expression has a variety of meanings, depending largely upon where and by whom it is used, and whether "to do" or "to pull" is the accompanying verb. In sporting circles, "to do a brodie" is, generally, to take a chance, sometimes a daring chance. In theatrical circles and in some other instances, "to pull a brodie" is to produce a failure or a "flop," or to commit a blunder, or to fail or be defeated ignominiously.

Curiously, though the slang expressions are quite recent, scarcely more than ten years old, the source lies in an event, or series of events, of sixty years ago, especially one event that was recalled in the celebration of the sesquicentennial of the completion of the Brooklyn Bridge.

Steve Brodie, who was born about 1863 near the Brooklyn end of the great bridge that was begun when he was a lad, took great interest in its construction through the years of his boyhood. It is said that he was not too bright, intellectually, and that the imposing structure stimulated a zeal to acquire a personal fame or to do something that, to his notion, would celebrate the completion of the bridge. The height of the bridge from the lowest chord of the span is 135 feet at the center. Steve vowed that he would jump from it at that point.

Though completed in 1883, the bridge was not opened to traffic for several years. In the meantime, Steve Brodie's intention had become known among the frequenters of the saloon where he worked and eventually someone or some group made him a bet of $200 that he would not make the jump. According to the New York *Times* of July 24, 1886, young Brodie actually made the leap at two o'clock of the previous day, July 23, after eluding policemen on the bridge who had been instructed not to permit the hazardous undertaking. The account runs that he had been "well prepared" against injury by external applications of whisky and bandages. Friends were waiting in a rowboat beneath and picked him up as he returned to the surface; he complained of a "pain," which seems to have been alleviated by liberal applications of whisky, internally this time, and, though arrested for endangering his life, he suffered no further injury than a deflation of ego through a caustic upbraiding from the judge.

Two years later, according to the New York *Tribune* of November 10, 1888, Brodie jumped off the railroad bridge over the Hudson River at Poughkeepsie in the early hours of the previous day, a leap of 212 feet, as reported; this time to win a bet of $500. And the same authority stated that he had previously jumped from the Allegheny Bridge in 1881, a leap of 76 feet; from High Bridge, N. Y., in 1886, 111 feet; and from both the Covington, Ky., and the St. Louis bridges in 1887, as well as the Brooklyn Bridge.

But, fifty years later, when the semicentennial of the completion of the Brooklyn Bridge was being celebrated, no one could be found who could testify that any of these leaps had actually been made. Brodie had died when he was in his Forties; the newspaper reporter who related each picturesque elusion of the police for each jump and the subsequent "rescues," was a close friend of Steve's, and was always one of the "rescuers." Doubt was evinced that the "jumps" were anything but gags, hoaxes, for the sake of cheap notoriety; that each "jump," which might have been a daring chance, was actually a failure, a flop. Thus the lateness of the phrase and the present-day meanings are derived not from events that may or may not have occurred actually, but from subsequent suspicions and investigations that, fifty years later, threw doubt on the authenticity of those events and brought Brodie's name into contempt.

bull of Bashan

A person with a stentorian voice and powerful build is said to be a "bull of Bashan." The reference is to the Bible, to Psalms xxii, 12: "Many bulls have compassed me: strong bulls of Bashan have beset me round. They gaped upon me with their mouths, as a ravening and a roaring lion." The conquest of Bashan by Moses (Deuteronomy iii, 14), known as the land of giants, was a memorable feat to the Israelites; there are a number of references to it in the Old Testament. The size and power of the cattle were especially impressive.

from Dan to Beersheba

All over the world; from one side of the world (or the country) to the other. The expression comes from the Bible—Judges xx, 1— telling of the assembly of Israelites from one end of the country to the other to do battle against the Benjamites—from the city of Dan at the north end of the Land of Israel and from the city of Beersheba at the south end, and all points between. As far as the Israelites were concerned, that area embraced the world.

on (or *aboard*) *the bandwagon*

One who climbs or gets on or aboard the bandwagon, in the United States, is he who accepts or espouses a popular movement or cause that some leader has organized. It had a political origin—from the parades honoring a candidate for office and led by a loud band of musicians riding upon a large dray. For the effect upon his con-

 stituents, some local leader would, as the band approached, vauntingly mount the wagon and ride through his district, thus advertising his endorsement of the candidate. Though the band, the wagon, and the practice were long a feature in American pre-election politics, the phrase dates only from the second presidential campaign of William Jennings Bryan.

to whip (or *beat*) *the devil around the stump*

To evade a responsibility or duty in a roundabout manner; to get deviously around a difficulty. It may be that this old American expression is an offshoot of the familar "up a stump," which means in perplexity, in confusion, and which in turn came from the use of a tree stump as a platform for making a speech—one mounted upon a stump might well be confused and have stage fright. But if there was any connection, the explanation cannot be found now. In 1786, the date when the earliest record of the expression occurs, it was credited to Virginia. Possibly there was some allusion to the biblical admonition, "Get thee behind me, Satan," but it is more likely that it came from some folk tale once current in the South.

to teach one's grandmother to suck eggs

To offer needless assistance; to waste one's efforts upon futile matters; especially, to presume to offer advice to an expert. This particular expression is well over two hundred years old; it is just a variation of an older theme that was absurd enough to appeal to the popular fancy. One of the earliest of these is given in Udall's translation of *Apophthegmes* (1542) from the works of Erasmus. It reads: "A swyne to teache Minerua, was a prouerbe, for which we saie in Englyshe to teache our dame to spynne."

the goose hangs high

Things are propitious; all is well. This is sometimes regarded as a corruption of "the goose honks high," on the supposition that, in fair weather, the geese fly high and honk as they fly. The editors of the *Dictionary of American English*, however, report that they find "no convincing evidence" of such a corruption. Dr. Frank H. Vizetelly, in his *Deskbook of Idioms and Idiomatic Phrases* (1923), considers that the expression alludes to the one-time cruel American sport of gander pulling. As described in 1818 by Henry B. Fearon, in his *Sketches of America*, "This diversion consists in tying a live gander to a tree or pole, greasing its neck, riding past it at full gallop, and he who succeeds in pulling off the head of the victim, receives the laurel crown." Presumably Dr. Vizetelly thought that if the gander (or goose) was tied to the tree high enough, the contestants were assured of good sport.

to take for a ride

This may be jocular or serious; one is sometimes taken for a ride when he suffers nothing more severe than being kidded, made the butt of some joke. But in a sinister and the original sense the person taken for the ride rarely returns. The expression was of underworld origin, coined in the United States during the wave of criminality after World War I, when rival gangs of law-breakers waged warfare on each other. Anyone incurring the displeasure of a gang chieftain was likely to be invited by a henchman to go for a ride in the car of the latter, ostensibly to talk matters over and clear up the misunderstanding. The victim rarely returned from such a trip; his body might later be found by the police—or might not.

to let the cat out of the bag

If all the truth were known, our ancestors probably knew and practiced more sales tricks than the sliest and most unscrupulous merchants ever heard of today. Elsewhere is told one reason why a person was warned not "to buy a pig in poke," but, so it is said, there was another more potent reason—one might not get even a  stunted piglet; the wriggling contents of the bag, so like a lively pig, might be a cat. A luckless tradesman, who may not have examined each poke carefully that he had bought from a countryman, indeed "let the cat out of the bag" when the housewife insisted upon seeing the quality of the pig she thought of buying. Once a literal statement, we use the expression nowadays with the meaning, to disclose something that has been kept secret. Literary use of the saying is not very old, going back only about two hundred years, but in common speech it is likely that usage antedates that by another two hundred years at least.

to play to the gallery

To seek popular acclaim. The expression came from the theater, as long ago, at least, as the seventeenth century. Originally, the notion seems to have been a play that was written expressly for those in an audience thought to have been of lower intelligence and, hence, to occupy the gallery seats, rather than for the educated persons who had seats below. Later, the reference was—as it is today—to the actor or other public person who, cheapening his abilities, seeks the favor of the populace without troubling to exhibit qualities that might also win the approval of the fewer persons able to appreciate skill and artistry. In America, a synonymous expression, with the baseball diamond as its source, is "to play to the grandstand," that is, to play for applause from the grandstand; hence, to do something showy for effect.

to cut the Gordian knot

Gordius was the king of ancient Phrygia, in Asia Minor, during the times of Alexander the Great. He had, according to legend, tied the yoke of his chariot with an exceedingly intricate knot; so intricate that, by promise of the oracle, all of Asia would become the subject of whatever man could succeed in loosening it. When Alexander reached Phrygia, wishing to leave nothing undone that might inspire his army or impress enemies with his invincibility, he took his sword and, with one blow, severed the cord that tied the yoke to the chariot of Gordius. Thanks to the Roman historian, Justin, known almost only by his works, the legend has come down to us. And even now we "cut the Gordian knot" whenever we refuse to become enmeshed in a difficulty and use bold tactics in overcoming it. Shakespeare knew the term and used it in *Henry V*, Act I, scene 1. Therein, the Archbishop of Canterbury, pleased by the unsuspected virtues of Henry V, newly made king, says to the Bishop of Ely, "Turne him to any Cause of Pollicy, The Gordian Knot of it he will vnloose."

to swap horses in midstream

This homely American phrase is just our way of saying "to change leaders (generals, presidents, or what have you) during the course of an engagement (or at the height of a crisis)," and the point is always stressed that such change may lead to disaster. As a matter of literary record, Abraham Lincoln is credited with the utterance, though one historian of that period said that Lincoln quoted an old Dutch farmer, and Mencken reports the occurrence of the phrase some twenty-four years before Lincoln used it. The occasion of Lincoln's use was an informal address that he made to a delegation from the National Union League who had called to  offer their congratulations upon his renomination for the presidency, June 9, 1864. Lincoln knew that there had been considerable disaffection with the conduct of the Civil War and that many loyal Republicans felt that he had failed as the commander in chief. Hence, in his speech, he said, "I do not allow myself to suppose that either the Convention or the League have concluded to decide that I am either the greatest or the best man in America, but rather they have concluded it is not best to swap horses while crossing the river, and have further concluded that I am not so poor a horse that they might not make a botch of it in trying to swap."

halcyon days

The seven days preceding and the seven days following the shortest day of the year, believed by the ancients always to be windless and calm; hence, any protracted time of peace and serenity, rest and rejoicing. According to Greek legend, Halcyone and her husband, whom she had found drowned upon the shore, were turned into birds by the gods and were thereafter known as halcyons, or, as we call them, kingfishers. Their nests were believed to be built upon the sea, and the gods decreed that whenever these birds wished to build their nests, the sea should remain perfectly calm and unruffled. They made their nests, according to Pliny, during the seven days preceding the winter solstice and brooded upon their eggs during the next seven days. The same writer says that the nests, as they floated upon the water, resembled a kind of ball, not unlike a large sponge. The legend, of course, and Pliny's description are equally fanciful, but they were believed as late as 1398 when John de Trevisa, in translating *De Proprietatibus Rerum* by Bartholomæus, wrote, "In the cliffe of a ponde of Occean, Alicion, a see foule, in wynter maketh her neste and layeth egges in vii days and sittyth on brood seuen dayes."

to nail to the counter

It is usually a lie, a canard, or the like that one, emphatically, "nails to the counter." By this, the one who does the figurative nailing means that he declares or asserts publicly that the statement is false, definitely and wholly false. The allusion is to a former practice of storekeepers when taken in by a spurious coin. Such a coin, when found to be bad, was nailed to the counter where it could be handily compared with others of similar appearance when offered. Oliver

Wendell Holmes, the doctor and poet, is quoted as the first literary user of the expression in the figurative sense. In one of his serious works, published in 1842, he speaks of certain alleged facts that "have been suffered to pass current so long that it is time they should be nailed to the counter."

to read the riot act

When Bill, or even his sister, stays out too late, or drives too fast, or commits some other indiscretion which, we feel, requires stern reproof or threat of severe punishment upon repetition, we "read the riot act"; that is, we administer a severe scolding and a warning. The allusion is to the actual Riot Act decreed in 1716 by George I of England. That act, to quote *The Encyclopedia Britannica, Eleventh Edition*, "makes it the duty of a justice, sheriff, mayor, or other authority, wherever twelve persons or more are unlawfully, riotously and tumultuously assembled together, to the disturbance of the public peace, to resort to the place of such assembly and read the following proclamation: 'Our Sovereign Lord the King chargeth and commandeth all persons being assembled immediately to disperse themselves, and peaceably to depart to their habitations or to their lawful business, upon the pains contained in the act made in the first year of King George for preventing tumultuous and riotous assemblies. God save the King.' " The penalty for disobedience was penal servitude for life or for not less than three years or imprisonment with or without hard labor for not more than two years.

plain as a pikestaff

We use this now to mean thoroughly obvious, quite clear; but originally it meant bare and unadorned. The reference was to the metal-shod staff or walking stick used by pilgrims or foot travelers during the fifteenth and sixteenth centuries. That staff was for service, rather than for show, and was polished plain and smooth through use. In some localities, the expression was "plain as a packstaff," with reference to the equally smooth staff on which a peddler carried his pack. Both phrases are found at about the same time in early sixteenth-century literature.

to upset the apple cart

To ruin one's carefully laid plans; to turn things topsy-turvey; to halt a procedure as effectively as a farmer would be halted if, on his way to market with a load of apples, his cart were to be overturned. The Romans had a similar saying, minus the apples, and with the same meaning: "Perii, plaustrum perculi! (I am undone, I have  upset my cart!)" Probably the expression came into English through the translation of some witty eighteenth-century schoolboy who, when called upon to read the line in Plautus' *Epidicus*, where it occurs, called it an apple cart to be more effective. If so, the new rendition became popular almost simultaneously on both sides of the Atlantic, for concurrently with the record in England by Francis Grose in 1796 in the second edition of his *Classical Dictionary of the Vulgar Tongue*, it was used in New Hampshire by the political satirist, Thomas G. Fessenden, in one of his poetic attacks on Jefferson's policies.

to cook one's goose

To frustrate one; to ruin one's schemes or plans. As far as can be positively determined, the expression with this meaning is no older than the middle of the last century. It appeared then in a doggerel current in England at the time when Pope Pius IX, sought to re-establish the Catholic hierarchy in England through the appointment of the English cardinal, Nicholas Wiseman. The doggerel, expressive of high resentment in some quarters against the action, ran, in part:

> *If they come here we'll cook their goose,*
> *The Pope and Cardinal Wiseman.*

This does not explain the origin of our phrase, however. Both in Walsh's *Handbook of Literary Curiosities* and Brewer's *Dictionary of Phrase and Fable*, it is attributed to an incident that occurred during the reign of the "Mad King of Sweden," Eric XIV, that began in 1560. Walsh's account is the more interesting because it purports to be in the wording of some anonymous ancient chronicler. It reads: "The Kyng of Swedland coming to a towne of his enemyes with very little company, his enemyes, to slyghte his forces, did hang out a goose for him to shoote, but perceiving before nyghte that these fewe soldiers had invaded and sette their chiefe houlds on fire, they demanded of him what his intent was, to whom he replyed, 'To cook your goose.' "

To my notion, however, it would be simpler to look for the origin in the old folk tale, "The Goose that laid the Golden Eggs." Here, you will recall, the couple to whom the goose belonged became so eager to amass great wealth quickly that they couldn't wait for the daily golden egg from their rare bird, so they killed her in order to lay hands more quickly upon the eggs still within her body. Their aims were frustrated, you may remember, because the unlaid eggs had not yet turned to gold. So all they had was a dead goose which, if their former habits of frugality had not been wholly lost, they undoubtedly plucked and cooked for dinner. Both literally and figuratively, their goose was cooked.

a kettle of fish

Prefaced by some such adjective as fine, nice, or pretty, this is an ironic way of saying a terrible mess. It was so used by the British novelists, Samuel Richardson, in *Pamela*, and Henry Fielding, in *Joseph Andrews*, back in 1742. The expression is assumed to have arisen from a custom of the gentry residing along the river Tweed. According to a writer who toured the region in 1785, "It is customary for the gentlemen who live near the Tweed to entertain their neighbors and friends with a Fête Champêtre, which they call giving 'a kettle of fish.' Tents or marquees are pitched near the flowery  banks of the river . . . a fire is kindled, and live salmon thrown into boiling kettles." Scott mentioned such a picnic in *St. Ronan's Well*. Probably there were times when things went awry with the kettle of fish; maybe the chowder burned, or someone forgot the salt, or maybe the kettle would overturn. In any such instance the picnic would be ruined, the "kettle of fish" would be a sad failure.

lock, stock, and barrel

Today we would say, "the whole works," and mean the same thing. The expression is of American origin and, though the earliest literary record appears to be in one of T. C. Haliburton's "Sam Slick" stories, it probably goes back at least to the American Revolution. The three items of which the expression is comprised are the three essential components of a gun—the barrel, the stock, and the lock, or firing mechanism. In other words, the entire gun; the whole thing; the entirety.

to bury the hatchet

To settle one's differences and take up friendly relations. We in America are accustomed to think of this as an Indian custom; that it was a literal action, after the cessation of hostilities against the whites or a neighboring tribe, with considerable ceremony to bury a war tomahawk. I think, however, that the practice was merely attributed to the Indian, for I have not been able to find that there was any such ritual or saying among the Indians of North America. However, a similar saying has been extant in English speech since the early fourteenth century, more than a century and a half before the discoveries of Columbus. It was, "to hang up the hatchet," and it had the same meaning as the phrase that we attribute to the Indians. The earliest record, according to Apperson, is in a political song of about 1327: "Hang up thyn hachet ant thi knyf." The substitution of "bury" for "hang" did not take place until the eighteenth century.

Catherine wheel

In some localities such a piece of fireworks as this is called a pin-wheel, because the smaller sizes may be pinned to a tree or post where they rotate merrily, giving forth showers of sparks. The large sizes used in big celebrations have the more exalted name. Little is definitely known of the girl or woman whose name is associated with this pyrotechnic device, beyond the tradition that she lived during the reign of Maximinus in the fourth century. According to legend, she was born of a noble family in Alexandria and while a young girl embraced Christianity, becoming an ardent evangelist. The emperor, antagonistic to the spread of this belief, it is said, determined that her powers of eloquence be silenced; but those charged with showing her the falsity of her beliefs were themselves converted to her faith. This so aroused the emperor that he condemned them to be burned at the stake and Catherine to be torn to pieces upon an especially devised wheel, a wheel armed along its rim with curved spikes which, as the wheel revolved, would tear the flesh from its victim. But, so the legend runs, as the torture was about to begin, a bolt of lightning shattered the wheel and severed the cords by which the maiden was bound. The miracle, however, failed to sway the emperor from his course, for he then had her scourged and beheaded. She became one of the earliest of the Roman Catholic saints; numerous chapels have been dedicated to her, and statues that honor her usually show also a representation of the wheel as her symbol. This symbol, with curved spikes on the rim, appeared often in medieval heraldry; and the name "Catherine wheel" is also sometimes applied, in church architecture, to the wheel or rose window.

to bell the cat

In figurative use this means to undertake a hazardous mission that may cost one his neck or his job, as when acting as ringleader in telling the boss that the working conditions are unpleasant. It alludes to an ancient fable of mice and a cat. A family of mice, finding that fear of the cat so disturbs them that they are unable to forage for food, holds a meeting to discuss their problem and figure out some course of action. After a prolonged session it is decided that the  best solution is to get a brass bell and, in the words of Langland, in *The Vision of Piers Plowman*, "hangen it vp-on the cattes hals (neck); thanne here we mowen (we may hear) where he ritt (scratch) or rest." All agree upon the excellence of the scheme and they beam with pleasure over their cleverness. But the meeting is thrown into consternation when one graybeard steps forward, calls for attention, and solemnly asks the question, "Who will bell the cat?"

An historic use of the phrase occurred in Scotland in 1482. The king, James III, influenced by certain of his courtiers, imprisoned his two brothers. A loyal group of the nobles of Scotland determined, however, even at the risk of displeasing their sovereign, to save him from his courtiers by seizing them and turning them over to the assassin. They found that it would be necessary actually to enter the king's presence in order to apprehend the false counselors, but the Earl of Angus offered to run the grave risk and said, "I will bell the cat." The deed was accomplished, but, so history says, one of the king's brothers had already died or had been murdered, and the other had fled to France.

in the nick of time

It means, of course, at the critical or precise moment; just at the instant when our hero was saved at the last moment from onrushing death, for example. The expression is about three centuries old, formed when someone added the redundant "of time" to the older expression, "in the nick," which meant the same thing. A nick is a groove, a notch, as made with a sharp knife when one cuts a V in a stick of wood. Nothing could express precision more accurately than a notch so formed, especially when applied to time.

Procrustean bed (bed of Procrustes)

In Greek legend, Procrustes was a notorious robber, living on the roadside near Eleusis. Unsuspecting weary travelers who stopped at his home for an overnight rest were always accommodated. But Procrustes had two beds, one that was overly long and one that was unusually short. A tall traveler would be given the short bed, whereas a short traveler would be shown to the long bed. But to overcome these discrepancies, the inhumane bandit merely chopped off the legs of his tall guest or stretched the bones of the short one. In either case the victim died, but Procrustes had fitted his guests to his beds. Thus, in figurative use, we speak of a Procrustean bed, or bed of Procrustes, when we must use violent or arbitrary measures in an attempt to fit something to a condition with which it does not readily conform.

like a bull in a china shop

Like one, who, heedless of physical damage or the personal feelings of anyone, shoulders his way through delicate situations. This is another of the numerous idiomatic waifs in English literature which, like Topsy, apparently "jus' growed." One would expect a story back of the saying, but none has been found. The nearest is one from Aesop's fables, "The Ass in the  Shop of the Potter," in which the Ass, pictured as clumsy and stupid, breaks most of the earthen pots in the shop, awkwardly knocking down two while trying not to bump into a third. The expression is not an old one; no earlier literary record has been found than in Marryat's *Jacob Faithful*, written in 1834—but I suspect that its origin may have been a cartoon, an illustration of some sort poking fun at some British political event of the early nineteenth century. This cartoon, I would surmise, depicted "John Bull" in the role of the Ass and, with reference to some episode or event connected with British trade with China, threatening the destruction of a "China" shop, substituted by the artist for the potter's shop of the fable. The episode may have been the failure of Lord Amherst's diplomatic mission to China in 1816, or the events may have had to do with the termination of the monopoly by the East India Company, in 1834, of trade with China. The cartoonist may have been some such political satirist as George Cruikshank, or the earlier caricaturists, James Gillray or Thomas Rowlandson.

apple of discord

Anything that furnishes a cause for disagreement. The allusion is to an oft-told Greek legend which relates that Eris, goddess of discord, angry because she alone of all the goddesses had not been invited to the wedding of Peleus, king of Thessaly, and the sea nymph, Thetis, threw a golden apple among the guests, upon which she had written, "For the fairest." Hera, Pallas, and Aphrodite (in Roman mythology, Juno, Minerva, and Venus) each claimed the beautiful apple. Unable to settle their disagreement, they called upon Paris, son of Priam, king of Troy, to decide the issue. Hera promised him the sovereignty of all Asia; Pallas, all glory in war; Aphrodite, the fairest woman on earth as his wife. After careful deliberation, Paris made his decision in favor of Aphrodite, and as his reward claimed Helen, wife of Menelaus, King of Sparta, as his wife, bearing her off with the aid of Aphrodite. The result of the decision is amusingly told by Thackeray in *Roundabout Papers:*

"Angry, indeed!" says Juno, gathering up her purple robes and royal raiment. "Sorry, indeed!" cries Minerva, lacing on her corselet again, and scowling under her helmet. . . . "Hurt, forsooth! Do you suppose we care for the opinion of that hobnailed lout of a Paris? Do you suppose that I, the Goddess of Wisdom, can't make allowances for mortal ignorance, and am so base as to bear malice against a poor creature who knows no better? You little know the goddess nature when you dare to insinuate that our divine minds are actuated by motives so base. A love of justice influences *us*. We are above mean revenge. We are too magnanimous to be angry at the award of such a judge in favor of such a creature." And, rustling out their skirts, the ladies walk away together. This is all very well. You are bound to believe them. They are actuated by no hostility; not they. They bear no malice —of course not. But when the Trojan War occurs presently, which side will they take? Many brave souls will be sent to Hades, Hector will perish, poor old Priam's bald numskull will be cracked, and Troy town will burn, because Paris prefers golden-haired Venus to ox-eyed Juno and gray-eyed Minerva.

on tenterhooks

We use this now always in the figurative sense, "in anxious suspense." But a tenter is really a device used in the final processes of the manufacture of woolen cloth; its function is to stretch the cloth, thoroughly wetted in a previous process, in such manner as to rid it from wrinkles when dry. The olden tenter was an upright frame or railing of wood, the cloth being suspended from hooks along the upper rail and similarly attached to the lower rail, which was adjustable and could be fixed at any height by means of pegs. As an incidental note, it is interesting to observe that even in the days of

Richard III there were so many unscrupulous weavers who stretched their cloth so much that he had to pass laws obliging them to use none but public tenters.

Because of the construction of a tenter, especially the hooks along the upper rail, other similar devices were anciently also known as "tenters." Thus, the framework provided with hooks and used by a butcher was sometimes called a tenter. But particularly because the tenter was a stretching device and not unlike the rack in its construction, that instrument of torture was also called a tenter. And it was from this last device that we have our present-day figurative phrase, "on tenterhooks."

to peter out

The dictionaries say, "source unknown," so we'll do a little guessing. It originated in America; this much is very certain. Because it was known and used by Lincoln when he was a young man—a store in which he was a partner "petered out" when he was in his thirties—we know that it has been used more than a hundred years. It is possible that the expression originated through allusion to some certain man by the name of Peter, who, with an infinite capacity for engaging in new enterprises, never had the ability to carry any one to success; each in turn may have tapered off into failure. But I think it more likely that some irreverent American may have used it first in allusion to the apostle, Peter, with especial reference to his conduct as recorded in the eighteenth chapter of John. There, as you may recall, when Jesus was seized in the Garden of Gethsemane, Peter, flushed with devotion and eagerness, grasped a sword and rushed to his defense; but within the next few hours his enthusiasm had diminished to such an extent that before the cock crowed he had thrice denied that he even knew Jesus. At any rate, our expression could relate to the zeal shown by Peter, for in our use it means to taper off, to fail, to come to an end.

to fight like Kilkenny cats

In modern parlance, this would be an all-out fight, tooth and nail, no holds barred, a fight to the finish. There are three stories that have been advanced to explain the Kilkenny cats, and probably none of them is true. One is a legendary battle between a thousand cats of Kilkenny and a thousand selected from all other parts of Ireland.

In this battle, which lasted all night, the felines of Kilkenny were still alive in the morning, but a thousand dead cats lay on the field.

The second and more popular one refers it to a period, about 1800, when Kilkenny was occupied by a troop of Hessian hirelings. Some of these ruffians, bored by inaction, got the brilliant notion to tie a couple of cats by the tail, hang them over a clothesline, and enjoy the ensuing fight. One night, it is said, an officer heard the terrific caterwauling and started toward the barracks to investigate. Though warned of his approach, there was not time to untie the cats, so a quick-witted soldier seized a sword, cut off their tails and the cats dashed out of the windows. The officer, seeing the two tails over the line, was told that the cats had clawed each other until nothing but their tails remained.

But the third account, told by Dean Swift, is the most probable. It relates that the town of Kilkenny, lying on either side of a small stream, was populated by two warring factions in the seventeenth century—Englishtown on one side and Irishtown on the other. Friction was intense; hot tempers led to blows, and the turmoil was so constant that the town was prostrated.

"Gentlemen Prefer Blondes"

As far as is known, Anita Loos originated this expression when selecting it as the title of her book; but she may have taken the idea from an amusing book, *The New King Arthur*, which first appeared anonymously in 1885, but was written by an American poet, Edgar Fawcett. The book is a burlesque of Tennyson's *The Idylls of the King*, and in it Sir Galahad, "the spotless knight," is depicted as an insufferably vain prig. Vivien, a brunette lady-in-waiting to Queen Guinevere, desperately in love with Galahad, has sought vainly for the magical "face-wash and hair-dye," alleged to be a secret concoction of Merlin, the magician, for both she and

Galahad think that his affection would be fixed upon her if she were a "Saxon blonde." Frustrated in obtaining the concoction, she says at last:

> *Sir Galahad, canst thou never love me, then,*
> *If I remain brunette? I promise thee*
> *That no brunette of more domestic turn*
> *Has ever lived as wife than I would prove.*

To which Galahad loftily replies:

> *Hadst thou been blonde . . . ah, well, I*
>   *will not say*
> *What joy has perished for all future time!*
> *O Vivien, wildly, passionately loved!—*

Vivien: *My Galahad! Dost thou mean it?*

Galahad: *No, not now.*
> *I would have meant it, wert thou only blonde.*
> *Farewell, by blonde that art not nor canst be*
> *This woful barrier lies between us twain*
> *Forevermore. I shall be virgin knight*
> *Henceforth, with one long sorrow in my soul,*
> *And all my dreams and thoughts to one sad*
>   *tune*
> *Set ceaselessly—"She might have been a*
>   *blonde!"*

dog days

These are the extremely hot days that, in the Northern Hemisphere, occur during July and August. It used to be the popular belief that this hot period was given the name "dog days" or "canicular days," because dogs frequently went mad in such weather. Actually the name has an astronomical source. It is the period in which the Dog Star, Sirius, the most brilliant star in the constellation Canis Major (the Greater Dog), rises in conjunction with the sun. In ancient belief it was the combined heat of Sirius and the sun, while these two heavenly bodies are in conjuction, that brought about the sultry weather.

to flog a dead horse

One means by this to try to revive interest in an issue that appears to be entirely hopeless. "Dead horse" has long been used (for more than three centuries) as meaning something of no present value—as, "to pay, or work, for a dead horse," to continue to pay or labor for something that no longer exists, like continuing to pay the instalments on an automobile after it was smashed. The present phrase, however, dates only to the last century. It is ascribed to the British statesman and orator, John Bright, who probably used it on at least two occasions. One was when John, Earl Russell, sought the passage by Parliament of a reform measure, and the other was when his friend, Richard Cobden, was similarly seeking a reduction in expenditures. Bright favored both of these measures; both had at one time interested the Parliament, but that interest had waned. It was, as Bright said, like flogging a dead horse to rouse Parliament from its apathy.

to go the whole hog

From the evidence, this first attained popularity in the United States in the early nineteenth century, though it was not long before it was also being used in England. That is, the earliest printed use was American, in 1828, but that does not debar the possibility that it was not already well established in the common speech of either country some years earlier. From the first, the meaning has been to accept without reservation; to support wholeheartedly; to carry through to completion; to stop at nothing; to go all the way.

It is highly probable that the expression arose from a poem of William Cowper's—"The Love of the World Reproved; or Hypocrisy Detected." The works of this versatile genius were highly popular during his lifetime (1731-1800) and for many years afterward, though he is remembered now chiefly through his "Diverting History of John Gilpin." We need not here quote the whole of "Hypocrisy Detected," but the part which connects it with the theme of the present study runs as follows:

> *Thus say the prophet of the Turk,*
> *Good mussulman, abstain from pork;*
> *There is a part in every swine*

No friend or follower of mine
May taste, whate'er his inclination,
On pain of excommunication.
Such Mahomet's mysterious charge,
And thus he left the point at large.
Had he the sinful part express'd,
They might with safety eat the rest;
But for one piece they thought it hard
From the whole hog to be debar'd;
And set their wit at work to find
What joint the prophet had in mind.
Much controversy straight arose,
These choose the back, the belly those;
By some 'tis confidently said
He meant not to forbid the head;
While others at that doctrine rail,
And piously prefer the tail.
Thus, conscience freed from every clog,
Mahometans eat up the hog.

Each thinks his neighbor makes too free,
Yet likes a slice as well as he:
With sophistry their sauce they sweeten,
Till quite from tail to snout 'tis eaten.

It has been suggested that the expression had another origin, a monetary one, because, just as we speak of a dollar bill as a "buck," a shilling in England or a ten-cent piece in the United States was at one time called a "hog." Thus, a great spendthrift, one willing to spend an entire shilling or a full dime upon the entertainment of a friend in a bar, was willing "to go the whole hog."

a flash in the pan

This takes us back to the days of the flintlock musket, from the late seventeenth century until, roughly, a hundred years ago. In those muskets, sparks produced from a flint struck by a hammer ignited powder in a small depression or pan; this powder was the priming by which the charge was exploded. The process was laborious and, at the best, no more certain than, in these days, that a similar spark will ignite a cigarette lighter. Also, the powder had to be kept dry. But even when the operations worked well there was always the possibility that the priming or powder in the pan would merely burn harmlessly, just emitting a flash. Hence, anything that begins in a showy or ostentatious manner, and usually after considerable preparation, but which fails to go off in the manner expected, we still call "a flash in the pan," as our ancestors have done for several centuries.

sour grapes

Though sour grapes are mentioned in the Bible, both by Jeremiah and Ezekiel, the reference there is to the ancient proverb, "The fathers have eaten sour grapes, and the children's teeth are set on edge." Our figurative use of the expression, however, is derived from the story of "The Fox and the Grapes," in Aesop's fables. In  this fable, a fox espied some delicious looking grapes hanging from a vine. It was a very hot day and his throat was parched; the grapes were exceedingly tempting and, he was sure, were just what the doctor ordered. But, try as he would, the cluster of grapes was just out of reach. Each leap fell short by several inches, and the effort made him hotter and thirstier. Finally, when he realized that he could not spring high enough to get the grapes, he became philosophical. Even if he had been able to get them, he reasoned, he would have found that the grapes were sour and inedible, so it was just as well that they were out of reach. Hence today, we, finding that something that seems especially desirable is unattainable, may comfort ourselves with the argument that we would not have liked it anyway. To which an unkind friend may cuttingly remind us of the fable by the sly remark, "Sour grapes!"

a fine Italian hand

This expression is used to mean characteristic or individual style, and it may be in a favorable sense or an unfavorable one. Thus we may say that we see a certain artist's "fine Italian hand" in a piece of work, intending thereby to say that we are able to detect his handiwork by some characteristic feature. Or we may also detect the "fine Italian hand" of a politician who, secretly, is up to some sculduggery. But this is merely an example of how meanings are altered when the source of a phrase has been forgotten. The "Italian hand" referred to is the handwriting that was introduced into England from Italy some three hundred years ago which was "fine" in comparison with the heavy Gothic or Old English (or "black letter") handwriting of the preceding centuries. Germany was among the last of the nations to adopt the "Roman" type in printing and "Italian" handwriting, but we in America have never known any other style, except as we see it in old manuscripts or books.

to look a gift horse in the mouth

This expression or proverb is so old that its origin cannot be determined. It has been traced to the writings of St. Jerome, one of the Latin Fathers of the fourth century, who then labeled it a common proverb. The expression, or a variant proverb, occurs in French, Italian, Spanish, and other languages of Europe. The reference is, of course, to the bad manners displayed by one who receives a gift if he examines it for defects. Up to a certain age, the age of a horse can be determined by looking at its teeth; though it may appear to be young and frisky, the number or condition of the teeth may show it to be almost fit for nothing but the glue-works.

before one can say Jack Robinson

This means in a couple of shakes, two shakes of a lamb's tail, or, in plain English, immediately, with no loss of time. The expression arose during the latter part of the eighteenth century and, as far as anyone has been able to discover, it was no more than a meaningless phrase. No "Jack Robinson" nor "John Robinson" attained any prominence at that period.

a chip on one's shoulder

The expression, often in the form, "carrying a chip on his shoulder," is of American origin. It is used to describe a person who assumes an air of defiance or a truculent attitude, as if daring an adversary to strike the first blow. One cannot say when the saying originated; all we know is that it had become commonplace more  than a century ago. Possibly there was a connection between the chip that one dared another to knock off his shoulder and the chip of the ancient proverb, "Hew not too high lest chips fall in thine eye." By the late sixteenth century this admonition against peril had become something of a challenge; one who was fearless dared to look high without regard to falling chips. When transferred to America, this chip, which had become a figurative term for consequences, may have again become a real chip placed at the height of one's shoulder to warn an adversary against "hewing too high."

to go berserk (or berserker)

In Norse mythology, there was a famous, furious fighter who scorned the use of heavy mail, entering battle without armor, thus acquiring his name, Berserker, or "Bear Shirt." It was said of him that he could assume the form of wild beasts, and that neither iron nor fire could harm him, for he fought with the fury of wild beasts and his foes were unable to touch him. Each of his twelve sons also carried the name Berserker, and each was as furious a fighter as the father. From these legendary heroes the early Norse described any fierce fighter as a "berserker," especially one so inflamed with the fury of fighting that he was equally dangerous to friend and foe. So, since the nineteenth century, we have adopted the term and say of anyone in a furious rage that he has "gone berserk," using it synonymously with "run amuck."

not to turn a hair

The allusion is to a horse which, though hot, as from racing, has not become sweaty and, therefore, its hair has not become ruffled. The horsy expression saw literary use first by Jane Austen in *Northanger Abbey*. When used figuratively it means unexcited, composed, unruffled.

a song and dance

Typical of American vaudeville since the 1870s have been performers who, coming upon the stage, open the act with a song and follow it with a dance. In theatrical parlance, such performers are called "song-and-dance artists," and many stars of later life have been included among them. Because of the nature of the performance, however, the phrase has acquired two other meanings in common speech: First, thanks to the usual nonsensical patter that precedes the song, one is said to "give a song and dance," when he tells something or, especially, offers an excuse which seems to the listener to be nothing but nonsense. Second, thanks to the necessity for the accompanist or orchestra leader to start the musical accompaniment exactly at a prearranged cue, one is said to "go into one's song and dance" when, in the course of a speech or a conversation, he begins a statement or story that he has carefully rehearsed or has related upon previous occasions.

to take time by the forelock

The ancient Grecian sages, Pittacus and Thales, both of whom lived in the sixth century B.C., and the Latin writer of fables, Phædrus, who lived in the first century A.D., all advised the ambitious person to seize the opportunity or the occasion at the moment it was presented, so this saying has been attributed to each of them. It was Phædrus, however, who described "Opportunity" as having a heavy forelock but being completely bald at the back, thus implying that one could not wait until opportunity had passed before hoping to take advantage of its offers.

In agreement with Phædrus, English usage of the expression during the sixteenth century was, "to take opportunity by the forelock." The switch from "opportunity" to "time" came about through the personification by artists of "time" as an old man carrying an hourglass and a scythe, and, borrowing from Phædrus' description, bald behind, but having a forelock.

to eat crow

To abase oneself; be obliged to accept or do something extremely disagreeable. Though this homely American saying is not found in print prior to 1877, there is no doubt that it was in common use many years earlier. According to an account in an 1888 issue of the Atlanta *Constitution*, the incident which gave rise to the expression occurred along the Niagara River toward the end of the war of 1812. During an armistice it was the practice of the opposing garrisons to go hunting. While on such an expedition a hapless New Englander crossed the river in search of larger game, but finding nothing took a shot at a passing crow and brought it down. A British officer, hearing the shot, resolved to punish the intruder and came upon him just as the Yank was reloading his gun. But as the officer was unarmed he used diplomacy; he complimented the soldier upon so fine a shot and asked to see so excellent a weapon. The unsuspecting soldier passed it over, whereupon the Britisher brought it to his shoulder, covered the Yank, and berated him for trespassing; then, to humble him thoroughly, ordered him to take a bite out of the crow. Despite all pleas, the soldier was forced to obey; then, after a warning never to cross the river again, the officer handed back the soldier's gun and bade him be gone. But when the Englishman turned to go back to his camp, the quick-witted New Englander, now having the weapon, stopped him and ordered him to finish eating the crow. The officer begged and implored, but the soldier was firm; promises of money and gold were sternly refused; the Britisher, faced with death, ate the crow.

The incident became known, the story says, because the British officer went next day to the American commander and demanded that the soldier be punished for violating an armistice, telling his own version of the affair. When the soldier was brought in, the American captain asked him if he had ever seen the Englishman before. After several attempts to speak, the stuttering Yankee finally had the wits to say, "W-w-why y-y-yes, Captin', I d-d-dined with him y-y-yesterday."

sub rosa or under the rose

Whether Latin or English, German (*unter der Rose*) or French (*sous la rose*), it means in strict privacy, utter confidence, absolute secrecy. This ancient expression it is said, came down to us from the Greeks who, seeing the Egyptian god, Horus, seated under a rose and, depicted with a finger at his lips, thought that he was the god of silence. The concept was mistaken, however, for the rose was a lotus and the infant god was sucking his finger. But the mistake survived and gave rise in turn to an apocryphal story in Latin. This relates that Cupid, wishing to have the love affairs of his mother, Venus, kept hidden from the other gods and goddesses, bribed Harpocrates (the Latin name for Horus) to silence with the first rose that was ever created. And this story is credited by some as the origin of the phrase.

It has also been said that the expression was derived from some wholly unknown Teutonic source and that, during the Middle Ages, it was translated into Latin and thus spread throughout Europe. Verification of this theory is said to have existed in ancient German dining-halls where a rose was carved upon the ceilings as a reminder that whatever might be revealed by tongues loosened with wine should not be divulged outside. The phrase was known in the English court of Henry VIII, but apparently was not then so widely known as not to require explanation, for in a letter in 1546 that became one of the state papers is the passage: "The sayde questyons were asked with lysence, and that yt shulde remayn under the rosse, that is to say, to remayn under the bourde, and no more to be rehersyd."

a round robin

A petition or the like signed by a number of persons in such manner that the order of signing cannot be determined, usually as if the signatures were spokes radiating from a hub. This method of submitting a petition is supposed to have originated among British sailors during the seventeenth or early eighteenth centuries when presenting a grievance to the captain and officers of a ship. In those days the captain had absolute authority, when at sea, over the members of his crew and, usually, would inflict severe punishment upon any man who dared question any order or make any complaint. But a captain could not punish an entire crew who signed a petition, nor could he pick out the instigator of such a petition for punishment if he could not tell who had first signed it. The name is often supposed to have come from the French *rond ruban*, round ribbon, but the course is difficult to follow. In the sixteenth century, however, there was some device, perhaps a toy, or some trick practiced by sharpers that was known as a round robin. It is mentioned both by Miles Coverdale, in 1546, and by Nicholas Ridley, in 1555, and in association with "jack-in-the-box," which at that time was, to quote Nares, "a thief who deceived tradesmen by substituting empty boxes for others full of money." Coverdale, defending a religious ceremony, wrote: "Certayne fonde talkers applye to this mooste holye sacramente, names of despitte and reproche, as to call it Iake in the boxe, and round roben, and suche other not onely fond but also blasphemouse names." (In those days, "fond" meant foolish.) As the nature of this sixteenth-century "round robin" is wholly unknown, we cannot determine why it was so called nor the reason for giving its name to the sailors' petition.

higher than Gilderoy's kite

Gilderoy was an actual person. Just when he was born isn't certain or important; but he died, unmistakably, at Edinburgh, Scotland, in June, 1636. His real name was Patrick MacGregor; the nickname "Gilderoy" came from his red hair—"Gillie roy," a red-haired gillie, or red-haired laddie. But Gilderoy got into evil ways; he became a highwayman, and it was his proud boast that he had robbed Cromwell, picked the pocket of Cardinal Richelieu, and that he had hanged a judge. In due course he, along with five of his companions, was apprehended and sentenced to be hung. So especially heinous were his crimes that, according to the legal custom of the period, the gallows erected for him was very high, far higher than those for his fellows. "Kite" is a Gaelic word for "belly," sometimes used figuratively for the entire body. So, referring to our phrase, for anyone to be hung or to be higher than Gilderoy's body when it swung from the gibbet would mean that it would be exceedingly high.

In William Percy's *Reliques of Ancient English Poetry* is a ballad presumably sung by Gilderoy's sweetheart, one stanza of which runs:

Of Gilderoy sae fraid they were
They bound him mickle strong.
Till Edenburow they led him thair
And on a gallows hong:
They hong him high abone the rest,
He was so trim a boy. . . .

in two shakes of a lamb's tail

One who has seen a lamb shake its tail, sees readily that this saying means with no loss of time, for a lamb can shake its tail twice "before one can say Jack Robinson." Usage appears to be entirely American, going back a hundred years or longer. The probabilities are that the saying is a humorous enlargement of the older "in a couple of (or brace of, or two) shakes," a slang saying first recorded by Richard Barham in *Ingoldsby Legends* in 1840, but probably much older. This latter saying has been variously interpreted—as alluding to a double shake of the hand, two shakes of a dice box, two shakes of a dustcloth, or whatever it may be that takes little more time in shaking twice than in shaking once.

Garrison finish

A spectacular success when defeat seems inevitable. The expression is usually applied to a race, but is often used in connection with a political campaign or the like in which a candidate whose chance seems hopeless makes a strong and unexpected last-minute effort that wins the victory. Edward H. Garrison was the man to whom the term was first applied. He was a famous jockey, better known as "Snapper" Garrison, who died after a long career on the turf in 1931. Among the practices he is said to have introduced, according to an account in the New York *Herald Tribune* at the time of his death, was the so-called "Yankee seat,"—standing high in the stirrups and bending low over the horse's mane. The term "Garrison finish" was coined during 1882. In the Suburban for that year "Snapper" Garrison first demonstrated a technique that he had worked out. He held his horse in, trailing those bunched ahead, until the last furlong; then, in a superb ride, he brought his mount, Montana, past all others to win at the finish by a nose. It is said that he was unusually successful in pulling off this stunt in later races, taking a horse that appeared to be jaded to a strong finish. The first and later successes made that type of race a byword on the racetrack, from which the name spread into other applications.

on the bum

One may be feeling "on the bum" when he's not OK physically. It is an American expression, dating back fifty years or so. George Ade was the first to use it in print, but it comes from a dialectal English use of "bum," which for four hundred years has been a childish word for drink. The American phrase thus first signified  the condition one is in or the way one feels after overindulgence in drink.

But "on the bum" also means itinerant, living the life of a hobo. This second American use derives from a slang term which was current in San Francisco about a hundred years ago, or during the gold rush. A "bummer" was a worthless loafer; later, during the Civil War, a deserter who lived by raiding the countryside. Maybe the word was derived from the German *Bummler*, an idler, a loafer.

catch as catch can

This is what we say these days when we mean to catch in any manner that one can devise, by hook or by crook. But six hundred years ago when the expression was new our forefathers said, "catch that catch may," or, in the quaint spelling then used, "cacche that cacche might."

to lie in one's teeth

To accuse a person of lying in his teeth is the strongest of accusations, implying that the person is such a double-dyed liar as to be unfamiliar with truth. It is very old, traceable to the early 1300s, as in *The Romances of Sir Guy of Warwick*, "Thou liest amidward and therefore have thou maugreth (shown ill will)."

to set one's teeth on edge

The full proverb, as quoted by the prophet Jeremiah, ran, "The fathers have eaten a sour grape, and the children's teeth are set on edge." The thought of the proverb was that children would suffer from the iniquities of the father, a thought denied by the prophet, Ezekiel, who quoted the same proverb. This very ancient saying has nothing to do with our use of the expression, "sour grapes," but referred rather to the physical effect from eating anything as tart as unripe grapes, a tingling that seems to disturb the very edges of the teeth. Shakespeare, in *Henry IV*, gave us the figurative meaning that anything jarring to the sensibilities, such as "mincing Poetrie," sets one's teeth on edge.

apple polishing

The term is recent; the practice was known to your grandfathers and probably goes back to the Garden of Eden. Undoubtedly the wily serpent saw to it that the apple of the tree of knowledge looked attractive before offering it to Eve. The apple polisher of today is one who offers blandishments; one who, his father would have said, uses "soft soap," or what his grandfather would have called "soft sawder." The term got its name from the long-time practice of the schoolboy—rarely schoolgirl—of carrying a beautiful and tasty, highly polished apple to school as a "gift" to his "well-beloved" teacher.  Of course, it was nothing but a bribe, hopefully offered to one whom he secretly considered a lantern-jawed harridan, with the silent prayer that she would overlook any peccadillos that day.

to burn the candle at both ends

In the figurative sense this phrase originally referred to the wasting of one's material wealth, as when a husband and wife were both spendthrifts. We still use it with that sense, but our usual application is to the wasteful consumption of one's physical powers, as when a person tries to work all day and write a book in his evenings and spare time. It is not a new saying, and was not originally English, for Cotgrave, who died in 1611, records it in his French-English dictionary, "Brusler la chandelle par lex deux bouts."

soft soap

There have been many terms devised through the centuries for flattery, many of which have been retained in the language. "Soft soap" came into vogue sometime during the early nineteenth century, probably in allusion to the peculiarly unctuous quality of the semi-liquid soap that is called soft soap. Its predecessor was "soft sawder," or "soft solder," which was a solder with a peculiarly oily feel that melted at low temperatures.

to take to the tall timber

The twentieth-century version of the nineteenth-century "to break for high timber," and with the same meaning, i.e., to decamp suddenly and without ceremony. The original notion, back in the early 1800s, seems to have been literal, to make a break for heavily timbered regions so as to make pursuit difficult. The earliest "high timber" actually mentioned was, in 1836, along the banks of the Mississippi west of Illinois.

Black Maria

This is the popular name for a police wagon or van, the vehicle sent from a police station to pick up or transport persons under arrest. The source of the name is altogether traditional, not known to be fact, but generally accepted. The name is said to be the familiar sobriquet of a Negress, Maria Lee, who ran a lodging house for sailors in Boston, probably in the early 1800s. She was a woman of huge stature and, it is said, willingly assisted the police whenever her lodgers became unruly or violated the law. If this story is true, her name must have made a deep impression upon such British subjects as fell afoul of the law when guests at her house, for the appellation "Black Maria" was first applied to a prison van in London.

gone to pot

We use the expression now to mean ruined; destroyed; disintegrated. But the earliest English usage, which goes back at least to the sixteenth century, seems to have been literal, actually gone to *the* pot, chopped up into pieces, as meat, for stewing in a pot. There seems to have been a figurative meaning, too, in early usage, for a number of writers use the phrase with allusion to death, in some instances with the implication that the person dying had been the victim of a cannibalistic feast. Thus in one of John Jackson's sermons, published in 1641, speaking of the persecution of the Christians under Marcus Aurelius, he wrote, "All went to the pot without respect of Sex, dignity, or number." And Edmund Hickeringill, in his *History of Whiggism*, in 1682, wrote, "Poor Thorp, Lord Chief Justice, went to Pot, in plain English, he was Hang'd."

Other interesting explanations of the origin of the phrase occur. In *A Dictionary of Modern Slang, Cant & Vulgar Words*, published in 1860, the thought is advanced that the phrase comes down from the classic custom of putting the ashes of the dead in an urn. Brewer, in *Dictionary of Phrase and Fable*, says "The allusion is to the pot into which refuse metal is cast to be remelted, or to be discarded as waste." There is no literary support for either theory, however.

pope's nose

We also call it the part of a chicken that last goes over a fence; that is, the rump of a fowl. The name is said to have been applied to this tidbit during the days following the reign of James II of England when feeling was intense against the possibility that the British throne might again be occupied by a Roman Catholic. Some unnamed wit, during that troubled time, fancied a resemblance between the rump of a fowl and the nose of the pope—and the allusion stuck. But the witticism was not all on one side because, in America, at least, that "epicurean morsel," as Longfellow termed it, is just as well known as the "parson's nose," and has been so called since the early part of the nineteenth century.

namby-pamby

Henry Carey, who died in 1743, was both musician and poet. The song by which he is best remembered is "Sally in our Alley," though his original air for the song has been replaced by a tune composed by another. He is also reputed to have been the author and composer of the British national anthem, "God Save the King."

Ambrose Philips, who died in 1749, was also a poet. Both of these men were contemporaries of Addison, Steele, Swift, and Pope, living at a time when literary England was divided in allegiance between Addison and Pope. Philips, whose works were chiefly pastoral poems, received high praise from Addison, who at the same time ignored Pope's works in the same field. Hence, when Philips produced an insipid, sentimental poem addressed "to the infant daughter of Lord Carteret," Pope's scorn knew no bounds.

Now the nickname of Ambrose is "Namby." It is not certain whether Pope or Carey, who shared Pope's scorn, first hit upon the use of Philips' second initial for the reduplication, but Carey seized upon it and wrote a parody of Philips' sentimental poem under the title "Namby Pamby." Thus the term came into our language, and we still hold to the original meaning, "sickly sentimental; insipid."

bears and bulls

In stock market parlance, a bear is a speculator who sells a stock that he does not own in the belief that before he must deliver the stock to its purchaser its price will have dropped so that he may make a profit on the transaction. A bull, on the other hand, is optimistic of future rises in the value of a stock; he buys at what he believes to be a low price, encourages a demand for the stock, and thus expects to make his profit by selling at an increased value. (Both gentlemen may get stung.) The terms have acquired additional meanings, but these are the basic senses.

We must again go to Exchange Alley, in London, (see *lame duck*) to learn how these names originated. "Bear" was the earlier of the two designations. Even back in Bailey's English Dictionary of 1720, we find the definition, *"to sell a bear:* to sell what one hath not." The allusion here is to an old proverb, so old that it is in many languages, appearing in many forms. The English version was, "to sell the bear-skin before the bear is caught." Thus, in Exchange Alley, stock sold, but not owned by one speculating on a decrease in price, was formerly called a "bear-skin," and the dealer was known as a "bear-skin jobber." Later, although still two hundred years ago, the title of the dealer was contracted to "bear." The origin of "bull," used in this sense prior to 1720, is not positively known. It is probable, however, that it was adopted through the long association of the two words, bear and bull, in the old English sports of bearbaiting and bullbaiting.

in one's black book

This has now no more sinister meaning than a loss of favor, more or less temporarily; but at one time to have one's name entered upon an official book with a black cover was a very serious matter. The first of these historic books of ill omen was one compiled in the reign of Henry VIII. It was a report on the English monasteries, and as Henry was desirous of seizing the papal authority and revenue in England, each of the monasteries listed in the report was conveniently found to be a seat of "manifest sin, vicious, carnal, and abominable living." It was not difficult to induce Parliament, therefore, to dissolve these monasteries and, in 1536, to assign their property to the king.

The saying itself arose from that historic incident, but there were later "black books" in which records were kept of persons charged with violations of the law or of misdemeanors. One of these, in the eighteenth century, was a university list of students under censure; another, in the British army, named the officers who had committed offenses; another, begun some seventy-odd years ago and annually extended, listed the habitual criminals of England. So, although we may lightly say that we are in someone's "black book," it might be discreet to avoid the expression when a police officer is about.

Incidentally, a "black list" has a similar connotation. This is a list of persons who are under suspicion. Popular use of the expression apparently goes back to the reign of Charles II of England, with reference to the list of persons implicated in the trial, condemnation, and execution of his father, Charles I. Clemency was ultimately extended to all but the fifty-eight men who, as judges, condemned his father to death.

three sheets in the wind

This means, of course, pretty drunk, reeling from too much indulgence in strong drink, somewhat more tipsy than "half-seas over." Like many other common expressions, the phrase dates back to the times when ocean navigation was entirely by sail. But in nautical use, a sheet is not a sail, as landsmen are accustomed to suppose, but the rope or chain attached to the lower corner of a sail by which the angle of the sail is controlled. In a strong wind the sheet may be loosened, and is then said to be "in the wind," flapping and fluttering without restraint. If all three sheets are loose, as in a gale, the vessel staggers and reels very much like a drunken person.

to kick the bucket

At best, this is a disrespectful synonym for "to die." Perhaps if we used it only of animals, or especially of animals slaughtered for food we might approach a literal meaning and the phrase would lose its humorous concept. The evidence on the original meaning is slight and perhaps future etymologists will find other and stronger clues for another interpretation. This evidence is that "bucket," in this phrase, refers to a beam or yoke on which anything may be hung or carried. This evidence is supported by Levin's *Dictionarie of English and Latine Wordes*, published in 1570, and also by Shakespeare's use of "bucket" in *Henry IV*, "Swifter than hee that gibbets on the brewers bucket." Further evidence appeared in *Notes & Queries* about 1860, in which a correspondent stated that even at that time in East Anglia "to kick the bucket" alluded to the way in which a slaughtered pig is hung up. His explanation was that "bucket" referred to a bent piece of wood placed behind the tendons of the hind legs of the pig by which the animal was suspended to a hook in a beam. Probably the dying convulsive struggles of the pig became the literal origin of the phrase.

It is interesting to note that a recent correspondent to *Notes & Queries* (April 19, 1947), who signs his communication only with the initials "C.T.S.," advances the theory that the expression comes from an old custom observed in the Catholic church. He says: "After death, when the body had been laid out, a cross and two lighted candles were placed near it, and in addition to these the holy-water bucket was brought from the church and put at the feet of the corpse. When friends came to pray for the deceased, before leaving the room they would sprinkle the body with holy water. So intimately therefore was the bucket associated with the feet of deceased persons that it is easy to see how the saying came about."

a peeping Tom

When we call anyone "a peeping Tom" we mean usually that he is a despicable person with a prurient mind. ("Prurient," to spare you a trip to the dictionary, means "inclined to lewd thoughts or desires.") A peeping Tom may be a person who peers into windows with a desire to satisfy curiosity; but whatever his purpose, he is not a popular person.

We have to go back to the eleventh century, to the story of Lady Godiva and her famous horseback ride, for the origin of the name.  Although Lady Godiva was a real person, who died about the year 1080, the account of her ride may be pure fiction. Her husband, Leofric, Earl of Mercia, it is said, levied a tax upon the people of Coventry which they found oppressive. His wife asked him to repeal the tax and, probably in jest, he promised to do so on the condition that she should ride nude through the streets of the town. Because the people of the town adored her, she had full confidence that they would obey her request that on a certain day everyone would remain indoors with the windows barred; in that confidence she rode through the town "with no covering but her flowing tresses." One person only, the town tailor, could not restrain his curiosity and peeped through a knothole in the shutter of his shop. Some say that "peeping Tom" lost his life through his curiosity, others that he became blind, but in any event his name has come down down to the present time as one who was too curious for his own good.

The story was told originally by an unknown writer in the twelfth century, about seventy-five years after Lady Godiva's death, and it forms the theme of a poem by Lord Tennyson.

at loggerheads

A loggerhead, in Shakespeare's day, was a person whom today we would call a blockhead—probably derived from an old word, *logger*, meaning heavy or stupid, plus *head*. But although Shakespeare used the term in that sense, the same word had a military meaning that was very different. In this sense it applied to a ball-like mass of iron, with a long handle, which, when heated, was used to melt tar or pitch that might be poured onto the heads of a besieging party or to set fire to an attacking vessel. The historical records do not say, but it is a logical assumption that the soldiers or sailors who were in charge of these operations with tar would, if the attackers came close enough, use their "loggerheads" as formidable weapons, bashing in such heads as came within reach. We can reasonably assume, therefore, that our present-day use of "at loggerheads," by which we mean "engaged in dispute," originated from the use of a loggerhead in battle.

to be on the beam

By this very modern expression we mean "to be on the right course"; hence, right, accurate, correct. It comes from the use of directional radio beacons established along lines of airplane travel. A continuous pulsating note emitted from the beacon is heard at its greatest intensity by an aviator when he is directly upon the course along which he should be traveling, fading off to dimness if he departs from the course to one side or the other.

living the life of Riley

There is excellent reason for the belief that the gentleman who gave life to this modern expression was given the name "Reilly" by his creator, not "Riley," but as he lived only in song and the pronunciation was the same no one will cavil over the spelling. The original song which seems to have given our present meaning—living luxuriously—was popular in the 1880s. It was a comic song, "Is That Mr. Reilly?" written by Pat Rooney. The song described what its hero would do if he suddenly "struck it rich." Some of the lines ran, "I'd sleep in the President's chair," "A hundred a day would be small pay," "On the railroads you would pay no fare," "New York would swim in wine when the White House and Capitol are mine." At the close of each verse there was a spoken line such as, "Last night while walking up Broadway the crowds shouted," and then the chorus would follow:

> *Is that Mister Reilly, can anyone tell?*
> *Is that Mister Reilly that owns the hotel?*
> *Well, if that's Mister Reilly they speak of so highly,*
> *Upon my soul Reilly, you're doing quite well.*

sent to Coventry

Why this ancient town, famed for the notable ride of the Lady Godiva, should have become a synonym for a place of ostracism, has been a matter of speculation for many years. The account favored by historians is rather tame. It relates to the Great Rebellion (1642-1649) in England, the struggle between Charles I and Parliament. Citizens of the town of Birmingham, it is said, rose against some of their fellow townsmen who were loyal to the king and sent them to the nearby town of Coventry, which strongly supported Parliament, where they would be unable to aid the king. These royalists were literally ostracized, sent into exile.

But in an old issue of Chambers' Cyclopedia we find a more interesting reason for the fact that "sent to Coventry" is equivalent to having no notice taken of one. This account states that the people of the town became so annoyed with soldiers who were harbored among them that fraternization with them was forbidden. A woman, for example, who was seen speaking to a soldier would be given the cold shoulder by her neighbors. Hence, it is said, no soldier wanted to be sent to Coventry, for he knew that while there he would be ignored by the townspeople. No date was given, but the reference was likely to have been to the same historic struggle between the king and Parliament.

with a grain of salt

Because this expression of skepticism, doubt, or distrust is so familiar to us in its Latin form, *cum grano salis*, we sometimes assume that it has great antiquity. Perhaps it does, for Pliny, in telling the story of Pompey's seizure of the royal palace of Mithradates, says that Pompey found the hidden antidote against poison which, all his life, the Asian king had been obliged to master. The closing line of the antidote read, "to be taken fasting, plus a grain of salt (*addite salis grano*)." But it is likely that this resemblance is accidental and that Pliny meant the phrase in its literal sense.

Our modern saying does not appear to be more than three centuries old. Undoubtedly the original thought was in humorous allusion to the use of a little salt to make a meal more palatable. Hence, an improbable story might be more readily swallowed by the listener if taken with a small amount of salt.

not worth a Continental

This is a long way of saying "worthless." But it is a good reminder of the early days of the United States, especially of the financial status of the country. During the War of Independence and until the Constitution was adopted, or for a period of about fourteen years, the Continental Congress was obliged to issue currency in the form of notes, but was powerless to levy taxes from the several states which would give those notes an actual cash value. These paper notes, because of their origin, were popularly called "Continentals." Because they were not secured by anything tangible, people were very loath to accept them. They became, or were thought to be, worthless, not worth the paper they were made of. The saying has remained, though in these opulent days we have forgotten that there was a time when a government note of the United States had no value.

that's the ticket!

It may sound a little far-fetched, but nevertheless it's true that this expression of approval had its origin in a mispronunciation of the French word "etiquette." Try it yourself. Put the accent on the second syllable. You will get "uh-tick'ut." Someone, perhaps a schoolboy, may have jocularly made a persistent point of such mispronunciation round the year 1800 or later in saying, "that's etiquette," that's the correct thing. From "that's uh-tick'ut," it was an easy and natural corruption to "that's the ticket," and the latter phrase acquired general use, making its bow into literature about 1838.

a feather in one's cap

To tell Johnny, "That's quite a feather in your cap," is to compliment him upon an achievement; he has done something to be proud of. Five or six centuries ago the expression was a literal statement; a man who had gained a distinction, especially upon the battlefield, actually wore a feather in his cap, or his helmet, as a token of his prowess. Later, presumably beginning in England during the reign of Henry IV, or early in the fifteenth century, any member of the English nobility was assumed to be a person of distinction, and feathers on the headgear, especially ostrich feathers, became a usual part of the costume of a nobleman.

It is said that the hunter's custom of taking a feather from the first bird slain in the hunting season and sticking it in one's cap gave rise to the saying. This may have been a Continental custom, but literary evidence fails to show its early use in England. It seems more probable that the English origin of the phrase came from an early deed of valor of Edward, "the Black Prince," son of Edward III. The young prince, who was only sixteen at the time, won his spurs in the historic Battle of Crécy, in 1346, when the English forces seemed to be so hopelessly outnumbered—nineteen thousand English and Welsh soldiers again sixty thousand French and allied forces. Young Edward greatly distinguished himself in the battle, and after the English victory he is said to have been awarded the crest of John, King of Bohemia, who was one of the illustrious French allies slain in the fight. This crest consisted of three ostrich feathers, and thenceforth became the badge of each succeeding Prince of Wales. From such royal precedent it is logical that subsequent valorous deeds would receive similar decorations.

to jump (or marry) over the broomstick (or besom)

The expression isn't very common now, though it is used occasionally by writers. The dictionaries are not very explicit, saying merely that it means to go through a mock marriage ceremony, in which both parties jump over a broomstick. During the times, a few short centuries ago, when marriage laws were not very stringent and not at all uniform, a man and woman might go through the formality of publication of the banns but might live together as man and wife without waiting for the sanction of the church. This, through a popular superstition of the times, was thought to be quite proper and legal if both parties jumped over a broomstick. But in Scotland, broomstick or besom now means a prostitute, and in France *rôtir le balai*—literally, to roast the broomstick—means to lead a dissolute life. So perhaps those who "married over the broomstick" did not always or long remain in wedded state.

the jig is up

As far as the word "jig" is concerned, whatever its origin it seems to have been a very old term for a gay and lively dance, probably a dance commonly known throughout all western Europe fifteen centuries or more ago. But in England, around 1600, "jig" became also a slang term for a practical joke, a bit of trickery.

When the victim of a practical joke discovers the trickery, he is no longer fooled. Nowadays he would say, "I'm on to you," or, "I'm wise." The old expression was, "The jig is up," and we have used it since with the general meaning, the trickery is exposed, the time for settlement has come.

half-seas over

This is what we say of a man when we wish to imply that he is pretty thoroughly drunk, not yet under the table and still able to get along, after a fashion, on his own two legs; not quite "three sheets in the wind." The English allusion is probably a reference to the likeness between the half canted gait of a man when intoxicated and that of a ship heeled over in the wind, with decks half awash. But there is also a theory that "half-seas over" is an Englishman's interpretation of the Dutch expression, *op ze zober*, which literally is "oversea beer," a beer from Holland that was particularly heady and strong.

as poor as Job's turkey

Judge Haliburton—Thomas Chandler Haliburton—has about vanished from the memories of most Americans as one of the earliest of our humorists; yet he was the "Mark Twain" of the early nineteenth century. Born in Nova Scotia in 1796, trained for the bar, and raised to the bench at the age of 32, he began sending a series of literary sketches to a Nova Scotian paper under the pen name, "Sam Slick." Sam, according to these sketches, was a Yankee clockmaker and peddler, with an aptitude for quaint drollery, subtle flattery (which he called "soft sawder"), and a keen insight into human nature. It is in one of these yarns that Sam Slick, finding  the need to describe someone as even poorer than Job, who, you may recall, had been stripped of all his possessions by Satan, hit upon the expression, "as poor as Job's turkey." He explained this by saying that Job's turkey was so poor that he had but one feather to his tail and had to lean against the fence to gobble.

Simon pure

We use this when we mean that an article is genuine, not an imitation but the real thing. Sometimes for greater emphasis we say, "the real Simon pure." The author of the phrase has long since been forgotten—an English female dramatist at a period when few women could make a livelihood by writing, least of all for the stage. Susannah Centlivre died in 1723; she was twice widowed before she was thirty, when she turned to literature for a living. One of her most successful plays, *A Bold Stroke for a Wife*, concerns a Pennsylvania Quaker, Simon Pure, who has a letter of introduction to the guardian of an heiress. His letter is purloined by Colonel Feignwell, who then impersonates the Quaker and marries the heiress. Later, Simon succeeds in establishing his own identity as "the real Simon Pure."

baker's dozen

This, we all know, means thirteen. But why? The answer appears to take us back to the thirteenth century, to the reign of Henry III, though it may go still further, to the reign of King John or even to the middle of the twelfth century.

A loaf of bread, like a Swiss cheese, can be made so as to contain more air pockets than solid material. This fact appears to have been known by professional bakers even in remote times. And there were some, it appears, who did not scruple to take advantage of it. Hence, bakers as a class were viewed with suspicion—suspected, perhaps rightly, of giving their customers short weight. In Constantinople as recently as the eighteenth century, it is said, a baker guilty of selling lightweight bread might be nailed by the ears to the doorpost of his shop as a punishment.

But in England, Parliament enacted a law in 1266 for regulating the price of bread by weight, though similar royal decrees had been issued earlier. The penalty for short weight was severe. But because it is likely that few bakers were able to determine accurately the weight of a loaf and did not dare risk the penalty, it became customary to distribute thirteen loaves for every dozen ordered by the vendors who marketed the product. Each vendor, in turn, cut off a piece from the extra loaf to add to the full loaf bought by a customer. This extra, or thirteenth, loaf became known as the inbread or vantage loaf, for it gave a vantage, or chance, to the bakers and dealers to obey the law, and a surety to the customer that he was getting full weight.

according to Hoyle

If the ghost of Edmond Hoyle were to listen to some of the heated controversies about various games of cards, all of which are settled amicably as soon as some one is able to say, "according to Hoyle, it is thus and so," he would be the most amazed ghost that ever returned to earth. Yes, Hoyle has been dead a long time—since 1769, to be exact—and the book that he wrote, *A Short Treatise on the Game of Whist*, was written in 1742, slightly over two centuries ago. But the book that he wrote was extremely popular and authoritative; it settled all the arguments over whist that arose in his day and for more than a hundred years, until Henry Jones, who wrote under the pen name, "Cavendish," brought out his *Principles of Whist* in 1862. Hoyle continued to be quoted, nevertheless, and his name became again authoritative when, in 1897, Robert F. Foster, a specialist on games of cards, brought it back into public notice with his book covering many card games which he called *Foster's Hoyle*.

to run amuck

We are likely to forget that civilization in Malaya extends further back than the founding of Rome, so when we ascribe the origin of this phrase to the Malays we must bear in mind that it is not an indiscriminate custom of the people, just isolated practice. The Malay word *amoq* means "frenzied," or, with extended implication, "engaging furiously in battle." Various causes may exist, but there seems to be an underlying temperament among Malayans that makes them peculiarly susceptible to fits of depression. Such a spell may be caused by jealousy, or by despair, and it may be aggravated by excessive recourse to opium or other drug. Its effect is to seize the victim with a murderous frenzy. He snatches a cutlas, or native *kris*,  and dashes out into the road striking at any and everyone he meets. A cry of "Amoq! Amoq!" goes up among the people, and perhaps before the madman has been able to do much damage he is himself killed.

English use of the phrase has become more figurative than literal; we may say that a person has "run amuck" when we mean no more than that he is engaging in an unreasonable attack upon the established social order.

to the manner born

That is the way Shakespeare wrote it—m-a-n-n-e-r, not m-a-n-o-r. The phrase occurs in *Hamlet*, Act 1, scene 4. The friends of Hamlet are amazed at hearing a flourish of drums and trumpets at midnight and ask him the meaning of it. He says that it is a royal drinking custom, "But to my mind, though I am native here and to the manner born, it is a custom more honored in the breach than the observance."

In other words, when you use the phrase, bear in mind that it refers to a habit or practice, a custom of the people; it has nothing to do with rank or aristocracy or high estate, as would be implied by the word "manor."

to run the gantlet (or *gauntlet*)

Every youngster knows that this means, nowadays, to run between two rows of one's fellows who will try to strike him, in penalty for some fault. The extended meaning is figurative, to encounter a series of unpleasant happenings. The original literal meaning, however, was sinister, often terminating in the maiming of the unfortunate man who was compelled to undergo such a form of punishment.

During the Thirty Years' War (1618-1648) the British forces observed a form of punishment used by the Germans which was said to have originated among the Swedes. In this punishment, the severity of which could be regulated, a soldier guilty of an offense was compelled to strip to the waist and run between two lines of his fellows, each armed with a whip, leather thong, or rod. As he passed, each was supposed to strike him upon the back. The lines of men might be long or short, depending upon the severity of the punishment to be inflicted.

The Swedish word for the punishment was *gatloppe*, literally, a running of the lane. This, taken into the speech of English soldiers, became corrupted into *gantlope* and was further corrupted into *gantlet* and, through similarity of sound, into *gauntlet*.

When Old World colonists began to settle in America they found that the Indians had a similar form of punishment or torture, with the difference that the victim, usually a captive, was not expected to survive the blows of the war clubs with which his assailants were armed. From its likeness to the European punishment, this, too, was called a "gauntlet" by the whites.

at sixes and sevens

This plural form of the expression is comparatively modern, dating back only a hundred and fifty years or so. The older form, "on six and seven," however, was so old and well known in Chaucer's day that, worse luck, he didn't bother to explain what it meant when, about 1375, he used it in *Troylus and Cryseyde*.

As we use it today and as it has been used for centuries, the phrase means "in a state of disorder or confusion; topsy-turvy." Explanations of its origin have been sought, but nothing certain is known. One writer tries to connect it with a Hebrew phrase that we find in Job v, 19, "He shall deliver thee in six troubles: yea, in seven there shall no evil touch thee." Another seeks an explanation in the Arabic numerals 6 and 7, which, he points out, extend higher and lower respectively in a line of figures than do the others; hence, that these two are irregular.

But it is more probable that Chaucer's use had reference to an old dicing game. From Chaucer and other old sources we know of one game in which to try a throw of a five and a six (cinque and sice were the old names) was regarded as the most risky gamble to be made. One who staked his chance on such a throw was reckless in the extreme, utterly careless of consequences. To hazard such a throw was "to set on cinque and sice," in the old wording. It is presumed that Chaucer's use, "to set on six and seven," had reference to a similar game. From heedlessness and carelessness in taking such a risk, the expression "on six and seven," later changed to "at sixes and sevens," may have come to denote general carelessness; hence, disorder and confusion.

the real McCoy

The genuine article; the person or thing as represented. The story is told, and has not been denied, that this expression had its origin in a true incident that occurred about the turn of the present century. A prize fighter who traveled under the *nom de guerre* of "Kid McCoy," showed such promise in the late nineties that the name under which he fought was also adopted by other lesser lights who lacked something of his skill and ability. It is said that a barroom frequenter, a little the worse for drink and in an argumentative mood, cast aspersions on "McCoy" as a prize fighter. Cautioned by the barkeeper that Kid McCoy was standing near, the drunk said in a loud tone that he wasn't afraid of any McCoy. When he picked himself up from the sawdust, after "The Kid" had delivered a haymaker, he is said to have amended his remarks to "any but the real McCoy."

grass widow

In modern usage, especially in America, this term is used generally to mean a woman who is separated from her husband by divorce; but this is a recent extension of an older meaning and is virtually unknown in England. Formerly, and still in England, a "grass widow" was one who was temporarily separated from her husband.

Thus, as recently as the days of the California gold rush, there were many grass widows in the eastern states, so many that they were also known as "California widows."

Various explanations for the use of "grass" in the expression have been sought. Some think that it may have had a coarse allusion to such a woman left to fend for herself, like a horse turned out to pasture. This is certainly more plausible than a fanciful explanation advanced some seventy years ago. In this "grass" was supposed to be a corruption of "grace"; that is, a grass widow was a grace widow, "a widow by courtesy." Suffice it to say that etymologists, though gravely analyzing this claim in all details, found it altogether untenable many, many years ago—perhaps one reason was because no one could find any place where anyone had ever used the term "grace widow."

But the term "grass widow" is much older than either the present British or American meaning. It goes back at least to the sixteenth century, and the meaning that it had then is still used in some of the rural parts of England. This old meaning was a woman, usually one with child, who had never been married, who never had a legitimate husband. It is supposed that, in the crude satire of peasantry, "grass" alluded to the probable bed in which the child was begotten, and "widow" to the unmarried state of the mother. This probable explanation is strengthened through analogy with terms in other languages. Thus, in Germany, Sweden, the Netherlands, and Denmark, for example, the provincial name for an unmarried mother is, by translation, "straw widow."

beyond (or *outside*) *the pale*

We use this expression now as if it had the same meaning as "on the wrong side of the tracks"; that is, socially unfit. That is an acquired sense. "Pale" means the region or district under the jurisdiction of a governing body, the part figuratively enclosed by a paling or fence. In English history, "the pale" meant those portions of Ireland, or Scotland, or France which, at various times, were under English jurisdiction. So "beyond (or without) the pale" originally meant nothing more than outside the district ruled by England. But rogues or even honest men sometimes preferred not to be under the jurisdiction of English laws and would "leap the pale," thus becoming an outlaw or, in modern usage, a social outcast.

a flea in one's ear

Taken literally, it would be most unpleasant and irritating to have a flea in the ear, and the original sense of the phrase carried, figuratively, an even greater unpleasantness. To be sent away with a flea in the ear indicated that one had received a sharp and stinging reproof or rebuff, often wholly unexpected. Modern usage has somewhat softened the force of the phrase. Now we use it to carry no greater meaning than that of warning. To drop a flea in one's ear often means merely to caution one against some procedure.

The phrase is very old. In English it has been used for at least five hundred years, and was then a direct translation from the French of that period. Modern Frenchmen say "mettre la puce à l'oreille," to put a flea in the ear. Rabelais, in *Pantagruel*, wrote it, "la pulce en l'oreille." Maybe the Greeks had a similar expression.

the $64 question

Back in 1940, in April to be exact, a new radio "quiz" program was started under the name "Take It or Leave It," with Bob Hawk as its master of ceremony. (Hawk was succeeded in December 1941 by Phil Baker.) Contestants, as usual, were selected from the studio audience, and each in turn as he appeared before the microphone had his choice of a series of topics upon which he professed a willingness to be questioned. Thus the topic of one contestant might be geography, of another music, of a third first names of famous people, and so on. The topics were divided into seven questions. If the contestant answered the first question correctly he was awarded one dollar, and he might then take his seat if he chose; but if he elected to try the second and did so successfully, the award was two dollars; if unsuccessful, he got nothing. He could stop at any time after a correct answer; but as the promised awards were successively doubled —$4, $8, $16, $32, $64—through the remainder of the questions to be asked, most contestants elected to continue, despite cries of "You'll be sorry!" from the studio audience. Each question was supposed to be a little more difficult than the preceding, and the final one, for which the award jumped from $32 to $64, was supposed to be the most difficult of all. This came to be known as "the $64 question." Thanks to the popularity of the program, the expression became well known and any question, as to a statesman, which was difficult to answer might be called "the $64 question."

to bring home the bacon

This may be used literally or figuratively; it means "to succeed in gaining the prize, or in winning one's point." Although there is still an ancient annual custom in Dunmow, England, of awarding a flitch of bacon to any married couple who can take oath that they have never once during the year wished themselves unmarried, it is not likely that our present phrase owes its origin to that scene of competition.

It is more likely that the expression has come from the rural American sport at country fairs of catching a greased pig. The lucky winner in this slippery contest is awarded the pig that he has caught; thus, literally, he brings home the bacon. But an old dictionary in my possession, the third edition of Nathan Bailey's dictionary of 1720, contains an appendix of "Canting Words and Terms used by Beggars, Gypsies, Cheats, House-Breakers, Shop-Lifters, Foot-Pads, Highway-men, etc.," and in this collection "bacon" is defined, "the Prize, of whatever kind which Robbers make in their Enterprizes." This would indicate that our present expression would at least have been understood, if it did not originate, in the eighteenth century.

It is also interesting to note that the compiler of this old collection considered that the phrase, "to save one's bacon," had a related meaning. He carries it in the same paragraph and defines it: "He has himself escaped with the Prize, whence it is commonly used for any narrow Escape." This is significant, for the phrase was not recorded before the late seventeenth century, and it throws doubt upon the theory, recently advanced, that "bacon," in the phrase, referred to the human buttocks.

like a Dutch uncle

In England, especially during the seventeenth century, the mannerisms and characteristics of the people of Holland were held in scorn. Thus *Dutch courage* came to mean cowardice; *Dutch comfort* or *Dutch consolation* meant "Thank God, it could be worse"; *Dutch bargain*, a one-sided bargain; *Dutch nightingales*, frogs. Even in America *Dutch treat* came to mean a treat in which each person pays his own bill. But the origin of the simile "like a Dutch uncle" is not clear. It seems to have originated in the United States, but whether the allusion was to the early Dutch colonists of New York or to the Pennsylvania Dutch is uncertain, for the expression did not appear in literature  until the early nineteenth century. The people in each of those sections were noted disciplinarians, however, and woe betide the unfortunate child who, having lost its own parents, was obliged to depend upon an uncle as a foster parent. The expression indicates a merciless tongue lashing, just the reverse of the discipline usually administered by an uncle.

to call a spade a spade

It means to call a thing by its right name, to avoid euphemism or beating about the bush. The saying is so old that what we have is just a translation of the original Greek. Perhaps it was old when Plutarch, in the first century A.D., used it in writing of the life of Philip of Macedon. But, although the expression is now firmly fixed in the English language, it is quite possible that the Greeks of Plutarch's time did not have the garden implement in mind in their use of the expression. The Greek words for "spade" and for "boat" or "bowl" were very similar, and it seems likely that the better translation would have been, "to call a boat a boat." Lucian, Greek writer of the second century, used the same saying, which Erasmus in the sixteenth century translated into Latin to read, "to call a fig a fig, and a boat a boat."

not worth a tinker's dam (damn)

Whichever the spelling, the intent is that the thing or matter described by the phrase is utterly worthless, of no value. In Knight's Dictionary of Mechanics (1877) we find the interesting explanation that a tinker, having a hole or the like to solder, erects a small barrier or dam of clay about the area so that his molten solder will not flow off. The clay, once its usefulness is past, is thrown aside. This explanation is ingenious, but it leaves one dubious that the practice, if true, would have been so conspicuous as to give rise to a household expression.

But we do have excellent authority for believing that the tinkers, mostly itinerant, were a knavish, drunken, and blasphemous professional class, during the reigns of the Yorks, Tudors, and Stuarts. Blasphemy was their most characteristic failing, and "damn" was probably the most frequent and most abused word in their vocabulary. From their mouths it became meaningless. Hence, to say, "I don't care a tinker's damn," or, "that's not worth a tinker's damn," merely adds a little intensive force to one's indifference.

fifth columnist

The expression arose in 1936, and came to mean, without regard to the numerical sense, a person who acts secretly within a city or country toward furthering the interests of an outside enemy; a secret agent. The expression is attributed to General Emilio Mola who, leading four columns of armed rebels against Madrid during the revolution in Spain, told the foreign correspondents that he had a "fifth column" within the city, meaning an army of sympathizers and active partisans waiting to assist in its overthrow.

to cut one's eyeteeth

To acquire wisdom; to learn the ways of the world. An eyetooth is a canine tooth, the third from the center in the upper jaw. The expression is somewhat literal, for the implication is that by the time a person has got his permanent set of canine teeth, has reached the age of twelve or fourteen, he has passed out of babyhood and has reached years of discretion. This wording of the saying appears to have originated in the United States, first recorded in 1870 by the essayist, Ralph Waldo Emerson, though undoubtedly long in use before that date. The British version, dating to the early eighteenth century, is "to have one's eyeteeth" or "to have one's eyeteeth about one." The usage differs slightly, carrying the implication of alertness against chicanery; that is, to use one's knowledge and experience in one's dealings.

to take French leave

We use this now to mean to take one's departure secretly or without authorized permission; thus, a soldier may be said to take French leave if he surreptitiously absents himself from quarters. But, despite the fact that the French counterpart of the expression is, "to withdraw as the English (*filer à l'anglaise*)," the origin of the expression is attributed to a custom that originated in France in the eighteenth century. The Emily Post of that day ruled that a guest who had a pressing engagement elsewhere might with propriety leave the function which he was attending without going through the formality of seeking his host or hostess and making a ceremonious apology for his departure. The latter, it felt, might lead to ⅃ general exodus of guests and be embarrassing to the host.

right as a trivet

A trivet is just a three-legged stool or table. The name, somewhat distorted, comes from the same source as "tripod," three footed. Anything that is three legged, as a milking stool, will stand firmly on any kind of surface. So the phrase, right as a trivet, means thoroughly right, perfectly stable. From the evidence of literary use, the expression is little more than a hundred years old; but the fact that Thomas Hood used it in 1835, and Charles Dickens put it into the mouth of one of his characters in 1837 indicates that it had long been in colloquial speech before those dates.

to go up (or down) the pike

We use this so commonly in America to mean up or down the road that we never stop to inquire the source. It is not used in England and is almost unknown there, and if we were to say "up the turnpike," by which we would mean just the same thing, an Englishman would be sure that we were daffy. He might say, "turnpike road," but would wonder at our current use of "turnpike," or our shortened form "pike."

Turnpike roads were common up to the middle of the last century. They were built by private enterprise or by a community or, as the great Cumberland Turnpike (or "National Pike") between western Maryland and southern Illinois, by a state or government. They were toll roads, the cost of maintenance paid from the tolls of those using the road. But what we today call "tollgates" were then called "turnpikes," a name that itself had long ceased to have any of the original sense. The first turnpikes were really rotating constructions upon which pikes or sharpened rods were mounted. They were effective barriers until the fare of a horseman or coach had been paid, and were then probably rolled or turned out of the way.

on the nose

This current expression had its origin in the radio studio. It means exactly on time. Those who have attended the broadcast of a radio program know that the director of the program stays within the soundproof control room during the performance. Thus he is able to see each performer and, via the engineer's radio, to know just how the performance sounds to the radio audience. His especial concern is to watch the time, for the program must run with railroad-like attention to schedule. In rehearsal he noted the exact intervals for each bit of the performance, the minutes and seconds for each song or musical number, for each bit of comedy or the  like, and has the elapsed time marked on his copy of the script. His assistant on the stage watches him for signals and transmits to the performers the directions he receives. If too much time has been taken up to a prearranged point, a dozen or more lines of the script may be dropped or the performers may be notified by gesture to speed up the reading of their lines or, if ahead of schedule, to slow down the reading. Tenseness subsides, however, when the assistant or the performers see the director place his forefinger on the tip of his nose. By that sign they know that the timing has been perfect.

Another sign that originated in the control room is made with the hand held up and the thumb and forefinger pressed lightly together. This is used to mean that performance is being rendered perfectly.

to leave in the lurch

This has nothing to do with the lurching of a ship or a drunken man. But we can't do very much with it except to trace it to an old French dicing game called *lourche*, which somewhat resembled the present game of backgammon and which was played some time before the seventeenth century. The player who was left in the lurch was apparently left far behind the goal, for in later games in which the name persisted it kept that meaning, as in cribbage in which *lurch* describes the state of the player who has pegged fewer than thirty-one holes while his opponent has scored sixty-one and the game.

hitting on all six

When first coined, this was "hitting on all four." It may become, as we adjust our speech to the progress of the machine age, "hitting on all twelve" or sixteen or other multiple of two. Whatever the alteration in the numeral, it means "functioning perfectly." We get it, prosaically, from the shop mechanic who applied it to the cylinders of the automobile. If the engine is running smoothly and efficiently, all the pistons in the cylinders, whatever their number, are hitting perfectly. We have given it a figurative sense, too, and use it, for example, in compliment to a person who, we say, is "hitting on all six" when he is giving a forceful talk or an excellent performance.

to hold at bay

Those of us who are familiar with Landseer's painting, "The Stag at Bay," know the meaning of the phrase; when facing a desperate situation, to hold it at a standstill. Despite the picture, the fact that the dogs are obviously barking or baying is just a chance double meaning of the word "bay." Our phrase seems to come instead from the French phrase, *tenir à bay*, which really means "to hold in a state of suspense or inaction; to hold in abeyance," or, literally, "to hold agape."

thumbs down

If you decide to veto a matter under discussion or to express disapproval of a person or thing, don't try to air your Latin by saying "pollice verso"; better just stick to the English "thumbs down." We know what that means and what the accompanying gesture is; but nobody knows exactly what gesture the old Romans used when they signaled a victorious gladiator to show no mercy to his opponent.

The present popular concept that "pollice verso" meant "thumbs down" is derived from the celebrated picture having that title painted by the French artist, Jean Léon Gérôme, and exhibited by him in 1873. But Latin scholars have advanced almost every other conceivable gesture except that shown by Gérôme. *Verso* just means "turned," and could mean "extended" or even "rotated." The Latin phrase has been translated, "with thumbs turned inward" and "with thumbs turned outward," in either case using the thumb as if it were a dagger pointing at oneself or thrusting into an opponent, much as we "thumb a ride" by pointing the thumb in the direction we wish to travel. The meaning, "with thumb thrust outward" has been stoutly defended.

From all these possible gestures one is reminded of the old children's game: Simon says "Thumbs up!" Simon says "Thumbs down!" Simon says "Wiggle-waggle!"

The Latin term for the reverse signal, to spare the life of the defeated gladiator, was "pollice primo," meaning "with thumbs pressed." Probably the gesture was with the thumbs folded into a fist under the fingers, and it may have signified that the dagger was to be sheathed.

on the nail (or *nailhead*)

This saying is used chiefly of money transactions, having the force of "spot cash," and we use it also to mean "now; at once." But it is so old that no one can be quite sure of the allusion. The same expression occurs in German (*auf den Nagel*) and in Dutch (*ep den nagel*). Walsh reports the occurrence of the phrase, in Latin, in a Scottish deed of 1326. These records tend to throw doubt on the claim advanced by Joyce (*English as We Speak It in Ireland*) that the expression had its origin in a custom formerly prevailing in Limerick where, he says, a pillar about four feet high, topped with a copper plate about three feet in diameter, stood under the Exchange. This pillar was called "The Nail," and a purchaser laid his cash upon the plate to seal a bargain. Probably, however, the pillar derived its name from the phrase.

An expression in French runs, *faire rubis sur l'ongle*, literally, to make a ruby on the fingernail; and it carries the figurative meaning, to drain to the last drop. Some have figured this out to mean that a wine cup is to be drained until no more remains than would make a ruby droplet on the fingernail. From this they argue, somewhat obscurely, that "the nail" in our expression meant the fingernail and that "on the nail" means fair and square.

to stand the gaff

We use this usually in the sense of "to take punishment," but often employ it for mental fortitude rather than physical, "to accept raillery in good spirit." A gaff, of course,  is a pointed hook on the end of a long rod and is used for landing large fish, or at least that is the instrument most commonly known. But there is also a Scottish and provincial English word, "gaff," which means noisy, insulting language; so it is possible that the expression, "to stand the gaff," may very literally mean "to take punishment, as from a steel hook," or "to withstand raillery, as from insulting remarks."

to spike one's guns

We use this now only in its figurative sense, to deprive one of his power, to make one's authority or arguments valueless. Its literal sense amounted to exactly the same thing, for the expression arose back in the seventeenth century and earlier when guns were fired by igniting the charge at the touchhole. If the touchhole were blocked, the gun would be rendered entirely valueless. And as the guns of that period, especially the siege guns, were extremely unwieldy affairs, almost immobile once they had been dragged into position, and had a comparatively short range, a sudden sortie by those under siege, if successful, would drive off the gunners. A nail or spike driven into the touchhole then destroyed the menace of the guns.

to pay through the nose

Legend has it that this saying originated during the Norse or Danish conquest of Ireland back in the ninth century when, it is said, the Irish peasants and nobles were compelled to pay their oppressors a stiff tribute or suffer a slit nose. We can only say, "not proven"; there is no historical record. Furthermore, the earliest literary use of the expression in English is not found before the late seventeenth century. The phrase means to pay reluctantly or to pay an exorbitant price, and it is likely, though not certain, that the saying originated among the thieves in England along in the sixteenth or seventeenth century, possibly in allusion to some practice among them of compelling a victim to yield his purse.

the land of Nod

We are apt to forget that this comes from the Bible, in which "the land of Nod" is the place (Genesis iv, 16) where Cain dwelt after he had slain Abel. Jonathan Swift, famous satirist of the seventeenth-eighteenth century, turned the biblical phrase into a pun when he wrote that he was "going into the land of Nod," meaning that he was going to sleep. It appears in a work of his, little known nowadays, *A complete collection of genteel and ingenious conversation*, (usually referred to as *Polite Conversation*), written between the years 1731 and 1738.

to be in the groove

This has no connection with being in a rut, for the current crop of American young people use it to mean to be exactly right, to fit exactly the mood or spirit. It seems to be a coinage of the jazz or swing era of music and to have been derived from the phonographic records of that music; that is, to the quality of accurate reproduction of such music through a good needle traversing the grooves of a record. The phrase is not more than about ten or fifteen years old, and, although applied generally to things that are functioning smoothly, its specific application is music.

to ride shanks' mare (or pony)

This means to walk; to use one's own legs, for the shank is the part of the leg below the knee. It has been a jocular expression for some two hundred years or so. Possibly it arose from playful allusion to a Mr. Shank who had no other means of conveyance, but more likely it was an invention of some Scottish wit.

funny as a barrel of monkeys

One monkey arouses a great deal of amusement. Two more then double the interest and amusement. If one were to release a barrelful of monkeys, we must suppose that their antics would become hilariously comical. The expression is common among children.

go to Halifax!

Most people regard this as a polite euphemism, probably American, for the blunter request, go to hell! But why Halifax? The explanation is interesting, for it goes back four centuries at least—to the manufacturing town of Halifax in northern England.

History doesn't tell us whether there were more rogues and thieves in and about Halifax than in other parts of England, but in the sixteenth century the people of that town had become so harassed by thievery that they had instituted what became known as "Halifax Law." This provided "that whosoever doth commit any felony, and is taken with the same, or confess the fact upon examination, if it be valued by four constables to amount to the sum of thirteen-pence halfpenny, he is forthwith beheaded upon one of the next market days." The instrument used for the beheading was an early form of guillotine, one that served as a model for the later Scottish "maiden."

As the seaport town of Hull, also in Yorkshire, had a reputation for being just as summary in meting out punishment to undesirable characters, these two towns became a byword among thieves as places to be avoided. They gave rise to the lines in the so-called *Beggar's Litany*, "From Hell, Hull, and Halifax, good Lord deliver us," for the three places of punishment were almost equally dreaded. Thus, in fact, our impolite order is not so much a euphemism for "go to hell," as a substitute with equal force.

to face the music

Our earliest record of this American expression is found, according to Bartlett, in the *Worcester Spy* in the issue of September 22,

1857. But a later collector of Americanisms, Schele de Vere, makes it earlier by saying that James Fenimore Cooper, about 1851, remarked that the phrase had more picturesqueness and was less unpleasant than "the Rabelais quarter." (His allusion was to the French expression, *quart d'heure de Rabelais*. Rabelais, according to the legend, traveling from Tours to Paris, had a bad quarter of an hour at a post inn when he found himself unable to pay his reckoning. He put up a bold front by accusing the innkeeper of a conspiracy against the king, and finished his trip at the expense of the terrified innocent victim.)

The source of "to face the music" is generally thought to have been theatrical parlance, referring to an actor who, however nervous, must come boldly on stage before his public; thus literally facing the music, or the orchestra in the pit below the footlights. But other explanations have been offered. Some ascribe it to military origin. If so, its first meaning may have been simply to take one's place in the line of assembly, facing the band. Or it may have referred to a cavalry mount which must be trained to show no restiveness when the band starts to play. Or it may have referred to a cavalryman dishonorably dismissed from the service who, it is said, when drummed out of camp would not only be facing the music of the drums but also would be facing the rear end of his horse.

jot or tittle

We don't hear this expression very commonly nowadays, though it crops up on occasion and we find it in the Bible, as in Christ's Sermon on the Mount. The expression as a whole means a minute particle. And that's just what it always meant.

Jot is a corrupted form of the Greek *iota*; the Greek letter *i*, in other words. The corrupted spelling, with initial *j* instead of *i*, goes back to the days before the eighteenth century when *i* and *j* were used almost interchangeably. The *iota* is the smallest letter in the Greek alphabet, scarcely requiring more than a wiggle of the stylus to produce it. And *tittle* means the dot over the *i*—a mere point. Anciently it meant any point by which pronunciation was indicated, just as we use *tilde*, a corrupted form of *tittle*, for the wavy line over an *n* in some Spanish words, like *cañon*.

So, by the expression *jot* or *tittle*, the ancients really meant something so small as to be scarcely noticed, not only the tiny letter *i*, but the even tinier dot or point over the *i*.

to get one's goat

This expression is now almost as commonly heard in England as in America, but although the first printed record of its use is as recent as 1912, one cannot say positively how it originated. It means, of course, to goad one into signs of irritation; to annoy, tease, exasperate. There has long been a French idiom, *prendre la chèvre*, (literally,

 to take, or seize, the goat; figuratively, to take offense), but the American phrase does not appear to come from that source. The tale that the expression derived from the one-time custom in the shanty neighborhood of Harlem, in old New York, of keeping goats, to the annoyance of the more aristocratic residents, fails to satisfy. There were too many other sights and sounds and smells in that neighborhood.

In my opinion, the more logical source is the small boy and his known habits of ridiculing whatever he may regard as an affectation. Turn back in your photograph album to the family portraits of 1890. Most of the adult males, you will notice, are wearing full beards. "Beavers," we would call them today. Now turn on to around 1900. Most of the full beards have disappeared; but now and then among your male relatives you will see that some were reluctant to part with all the facial adornment, needed something to stroke reflectively, and so retained a more or less neat tuft on the chin—a goatee, so called because it resembles the beard of a goat.

If you looked like a cow would your temper be unruffled if, from discreet distances as you passed, you heard, "Moo-oo"? That wasn't the sound your uncles heard; they heard, "Naa-aa-aah!"

to a T

We use this expression very commonly in the sense of minute exactness, perfection; as, the coat fits to a T; the meat was done to a T.

It is easy to dismiss the origin of the expression, as, I am sorry to say, some of our leading dictionaries do, by attributing it to the draftsman's T-square, which is supposed to be an exact instrument, but the evidence indicates that the expression was in common English use before the T-square got its name. "To a T" dates back to the seventeenth century in literary use and was undoubtedly common in everyday speech long before any writer dared to or thought to use it in print. But it is likely that the name of the instrument, "T-square," would have been in print shortly after its invention, yet the first mention is in the eighteenth century.

The sense of the expression corresponds, however, with the older one, "to a tittle," which appeared almost a century earlier, and meant "to a dot," as in "jot or tittle." Beaumont used it in 1607, and it is probable that colloquial use long preceded his employment of the phrase. Then as now Englishmen took pleasure in employing abbreviations and contractions, and I have no doubt that someone thought that "to a T" had a more amusing sound than "to a tittle," and thus introduced our current expression.

dead (deaf, or dumb) as a doornail

This expression means very dead, of course (or deaf, or dumb)—completely and absolutely non-responsive. It is very old, has been traced back to 1350 in literary use and was therefore probably used in common speech long before that, possibly for several centuries. But just why our remote ancestors conceived a doornail to be very dead, or deaf or dumb, is something that has never been satisfactorily explained. Todd, who published a revision of Johnson's English Dictionary in 1818, advanced the notion that the ancient doornail was a heavy stud against which the knocker was struck. If such a nail was used for that purpose, perhaps some old-time wit proclaimed that it had been struck on the head so often as to be dead; or another, after pounding vainly upon it without response from within, proclaimed it to be deaf or dumb. I don't know—nor have I anything to support Todd's theory. The earliest usage, as far as the records show, was with the adjective "dead." When "dumb" first appeared, in 1362, it related to the door only; as in Langland's *Piers Plowman*,

"As doumbe as a dore." "Deaf" did not show up until the sixteenth century, when it was applied indiscriminately either to the "doore" or the "doore nayle."

to fly off the handle

This Americanism first got into print about a hundred years ago, meaning, as it does today, to lose one's self-control suddenly, or, in popular parlance, to loose one's head. The latter was the literal meaning, for the allusion was to the head or blade of a woodsman's ax, which, if loose upon the helve, was likely to fly off dangerously at a

tangent anywhere along the swing of the ax. John Neal seems to have been the first to record the forerunner of the present expression, for the earlier usage was just "off the handle." Neal, a novelist from Portland, Maine, visited England when he was thirty, and while there published, in 1825, the novel, *Brother Jonathan; or the New Eng-*
landers. In this, speaking of a surprise attack upon an Indian village, one of his characters says, "How they pulled foot when they seed us commin'. Most off the handle, some o' the tribe, I guess." Our old friend, Judge Thomas C. Haliburton, who has already been quoted several times as the first to record some American expressions, has again the honor of being the first to use the full line, "to fly off the handle." This appeared in another of his "Sam Slick" tales, *The Attaché, or Sam Slick in England*, published in 1844.

forlorn hope

Things are not always what they seem, and this is one of such. What we have in this expression is really an English spelling of a Dutch phrase, not at all a translation. The Dutch spelling is *verloren hoop*, which sounds very much like the English "forlorn hope." But *hoop* doesn't mean "hope"; it means "troop" or "band." And *verloren* doesn't quite mean "forlorn"; it means "abandoned" or "wasted."

The Dutch term is of military origin; it designated a small band of soldiers, usually volunteers, who undertook some perilous expedition, such as heading an attack against the foe, or rushing forward the scaling ladders to breach a fortress. In modern military parlance they would be called "shock troops." But because casualties were very high and the chance of success always doubtful, "forlorn hope" has now the non-military meaning, "an enterprise having little prospect of success."

Philadelphia lawyer

Sometimes the phrase is embodied in a simile: "as smart as," or "as tricky as," or "as shrewd as a Philadelphia lawyer," or in such form as, "it would take a Philadelphia lawyer to figure that out." But always the "Philadelphia lawyer" is an exceptionally astute person and, nowadays, the implication is that he is given to somewhat shady practices.

Originally, however, to be compared to a Philadelphia lawyer was high praise. Prior to 1800 and for some time thereafter the City of Brotherly Love was the most important and the most beautiful city in America. It held, until 1800, the seat of the new federal government and was the financial center of the country. It was also the center of literature and intellect. Naturally the city attracted the best legal brains of the country, men constantly obliged to sharpen wits against others equally sharp and more than a match for other men with lesser opportunity. But when wits become too sharp, practices are likely to become less scrupulous, so what had been praise turned to satire as lawyers began to become less honorable.

all around Robin Hood's barn

Robin Hood (or "Robert of the wood," as some have explained the name) may have been altogether a legendary figure or may have actually existed. No one knows. The earliest literary reference to him is in Langland's *Piers Plowman*, written about 1377. He may have lived, according to some slight evidence, toward the latter part of the twelfth century.

But Robin Hood's house was Sherwood Forest; its roof the leaves and branches. His dinner was the king's deer; his wealth the purses of hapless travelers. What need had he of a barn, and how was it laid out if to go around it means, as the use of the phrase implies, a rambling roundabout course? The explanation is simple. He had no barn. His granary, when he had need of one, was the cornfields of the neighborhood. To go around his barn was to make a circuitous route around the neighboring fields.

a fly in the ointment

This modern version suggests that something unpleasant may come or has come to light in a proposition or condition that is almost too pleasing; that there is something wrong some-where. The older version was "a fly in the amber," meaning merely that something is as unexpectedly out of place as the fly that one occasionally finds embedded in fossilized amber. Possibly the substitution of "ointment" for "amber" may have been through association of ideas, for "amber" was originally used in the sense of "ambergris," and ambergris is used in some perfumed ointments.

from pillar to post

This means back and forth monotonously; from one thing to another; hither and thither. It is a very old saying, perhaps as old as the game of tennis—court tennis, that is, not lawn tennis. We who are familiar only with the rather new game of lawn tennis forget that it was invented as recently as 1874, whereas court tennis was certainly played in the thirteenth century and perhaps earlier. There is little resemblance between the two games, other than that both are played on marked courts, with a ball and, nowadays, with rackets; but lawn tennis is usually played outdoors, whereas court tennis is necessarily played indoors in a building especially designed for it. Rackets were not introduced until about the time of Henry VIII; previously, the game was played by striking the ball with the palm of the hand. The game was very intricate, even in recent times; the court laid out into side and end "penthouses," the roofs of which had to be struck by the ball, and there were "galleries," "grilles," "tambours," "*dedans*," and other structures involved in the game. Many modifications took place in the method of play, and at some time prior to the fifteenth century one feature of the game lay in some form of volley which, at the time, was called "from post to pillar," apparently referring to a post that supported the net (though a rope was used in those days, rather than a net) and one of the pillars that supported the galleries. No explanation now exists of the nature of that volley; but, because of the popularity of the game at the English court, the name of the volley passed into a common saying—always "from post to pillar" until the sixteenth century when, the original allusion having been forgotten, it gradually became reversed to the present usage, "from pillar to post."

Another explanation of the phrase has been offered. It ascribes the origin to the old-style riding academy, the pillar being the center of the ring and the posts being upright columns placed two and two around the circumference of the ring. The explanation seems groundless to me, and one is left to imagine a possible reason for having the pupils of such an academy ride endlessly from the center pillar back and forth to the surrounding posts.

to mind one's *p*'s and *q*'s

To take pains; to be careful and precise. More conjectures have been advanced to explain the original meaning of this phrase than upon any other equally obscure. Each has a certain degree of plausibility. The simplest explanation is that it was an incessant admonition among pedagogs to their young charges, warning them to note the right-handed knob of the *p* and the left-handed knob of the *q*. But if such admonitions were given to youngsters just learning to print the alphabet, why was there not a like warning to mind their *b*'s and *d*'s in which the knobs are also reversed? Another, of the same category, is that it was a warning to young apprentice printers who might be readily con-fused in picking out type, because the face of a type letter is just the reverse of the printed character. But here, again, the explanation is weak because the reverse of *p* is *d*, not *q*.

Another, and more likely explanation is that the expression originated in the old inn or alehouse. A customer, bent upon a convivial evening, would have his accounts chalked up against his final reckoning, so many pints (*p*'s), so many quarts (*q*'s). A little carelessness on the part of the barmaid might spoil his whole evening.

But other less plebeian explanations have been offered, dating back to the courtly etiquette of the seventeenth and eighteenth centuries when men wore queues. One of these refers to the probably frantic efforts of French dancing masters to instruct young gentlemen in the stately steps and deep courtesies of the minuette. The young men had indeed to mind their *pieds* and *queues* (feet and pigtails) to avoid loss of balance and to keep the pigtail from bobbing over the head or to lose entirely the huge artificial periwig.

Another associates *p* with the old word "pee," a kind of coat worn by men in the fifteenth to seventeenth centuries, now surviving only in the word "peajacket." This account would have it that "to mind your *pees* and *queues*" was a wifely admonition to avoid soiling the jacket from the grease or flour of the queue or pigtail. This explanation seems the least likely of the various ones that ardent delvers have offered.

to thumb a ride

This, like a number of other current expressions, is recorded in this volume for the convenience of future generations. You and I know that it means to obtain a lift toward one's destination by requesting it in dumb pantomime. It originated after the automobile had become so commonplace, around 1920, that pedestrianism almost ceased. If one wished to go a mile, ten miles, fifty miles in either direction along almost any road in the United States, all one had to do was to take up a wistful stand at the side of the road and point with his thumb toward the direction he wished to go. Sooner or later an obliging driver would be overcome with pity toward one so unfortunate as not to have his own car. In the long depression after 1930, many persons were reduced to this form of locomotion, and in World War II it became a virtue to share one's car and one's gasoline with others unable to get tires or whose rationed gasoline had been exhausted. By the end of World War II men in uniform were also sometimes able "to thumb a ride" on airplanes.

to cook with gas

This expression, at the time this is written, is classed as slang. It is included here because almost every other phrase in this book was, at one time, slang and eventually passed into literary use. Perhaps this will too. Currently it is used to mean to be strictly up to date, or even a little ahead of the procession, not out of date, as cooking with wood or coal would imply. Just why the expression should imply ultramodernity is not clear, other than that the use of gas is supposed to make a faster, hotter fire than wood or coal; but electric current as used in stoves is more modern than is gas.

to go haywire

Although this expression is wholly American in origin and use and is comparatively recent—*i.e.*, has gained popularity within the past thirty or forty years and is not found in literary use earlier than 1910—no one knows who coined it nor from what section of the country it first came to mean to be perversely unright, messed up, snarled, crazy, at sixes and sevens, makeshift. People who have never seen a piece of haywire now use the phrase freely and easily, as if it had always been in the language.

For the benefit of the uninitiate, when hay is to be shipped it is usually tightly compressed into a cubical bale, roughly two by two by four feet, and tied securely by single strands of soft, pliable wire about half the thickness of a matchstick. This wire is now generally called "haywire," rather than the former non-descriptive term, "baling wire." It must be removed before the hay is fed to horses or cattle and the best way to do so is by a sharp blow with a hatchet; the wire is then tossed aside.

Now with three or four strands of wire to each bale it isn't long before the farmer, liveryman, dairyman, or rancher has quite a mass of haywire on his place. He uses it for a thousand purposes, wherever or whenever a piece of wire may come in handy, or even in place of string or rope. He uses it to repair a broken implement of any sort, to wrap the handle of a split hayfork, to hold a broken strap together, to replace a broken chain link, to mend temporarily a piece of farm machinery, to guy a sagging stovepipe, to replace a broken section of wire fence, and so on and so on.

H. L. Mencken, in *Supplement One, The American Language*, advances his own theory of the origin of the present meaning of the phrase. He says, "No one who has ever opened a bale of hay with a hatchet, and had the leaping wire whirl about him and its sharp ends poniard him, will ever have any doubt as to how *to go haywire* originated." But with the highest respect in the world for Mr. Mencken's philological parts, and with first-hand experience with the diabolical punishment those leaping ends can give to a tyro, I think he has the wrong slant on the origin of the expression. It would partly account for the sense of perversity or craziness implied by the expression, but not the sense of disorder, derangement, general confusion, and hodge-podge that we also associate with the phrase.

Most farmers tolerate the use of haywire for temporary repairs only. They know that it rusts quickly, not only becoming unsightly but having little permanent value. But there are many farmers, loggers, ranchers, miners who are shiftless, who once having used haywire to hold a thing together, use it over and over again and never get around to making a permanent repair. Their machines, their tools, fences, gates, barns, sheds, and houses are patched with rusted haywire, more haywire often being added to a piece that has rusted out; haywire used to hold the paintless jalopy together; masses of tangled rusty haywire lying around anywhere. Such a disorderly, deranged, shiftless place has "gone haywire," and this, from observation of numerous such places in Colorado mining camps, Wyoming ranches, and Idaho, Utah, and California farms, I believe, gave rise to our expression.

INDEX OF PHRASES
AND EXPRESSIONS

Index of Phrases
and Expressions